This Book Belongs to the

If this book should ev
Smack its bum and

home to:

Becki Summers
6, West View
Beeston
Green
SANDY
Bedfordshire

Tele SANDY 82496.

CAROLINE BRADLEY

A TRIBUTE

MALCOLM SEVERS

Foreword by Dorian Williams

HARRAP · LONDON

First published in Great Britain 1983
by HARRAP LIMITED
19-23 Ludgate Hill, London EC4M 7PD

ISBN 0 245-54102-0

Designed by Michael R. Carter

Printed and bound in Great Britain
by R. J. Acford, Chichester

Contents

Foreword
by Dorian Williams

Caroline had not joined the Grafton Pony Club when I was involved with it. It was when I was invited back one day to present the prizes at their camp that for the first time I saw this pretty little girl of about ten who really stood out from the others. When I was told who she was and that she came from an unhorsey background I realized, even then, that she was that exceptionally rare phenomenon, a 'natural'.

In fact, the word 'natural' is particularly applicable to Caroline. I do not think that I have ever known anyone in any sport who, on achieving success, was so totally devoid of 'side'. She was always the same, took everything in her stride, went out of her way to be co-operative, was completely 'natural'. There were, I believe, two reasons for this: the first was that from the very beginning she had her priorities right. She wanted to succeed with her horses, was never afraid of the hard work entailed — which meant a great deal more than just riding them — but she had no desire for fame or acclaim: she shunned publicity, and with modesty that was totally genuine she always insisted that it was her horses that succeeded.

Secondly, she was a very shy person, almost introverted when she was younger. This meant that she always adhered to her own standards which she set for herself without any outside influences. She watched, of course; she learned and absorbed; but basically she was an individual.

Right from her teenage days and her early adulthood, when occasionally I used to see her out hunting or at some local equestrian event, she was always the same person. She was the same person when I was talking with her for a few minutes at the Birmingham International: twenty-five years after I had first seen her as a little girl. There are not many people about whom one can say that.

She was skilled, perhaps the most skilled lady rider in the world: she was professional, in her whole approach to the sport; she was dedicated, to such an extent that she exhausted herself; but always she was the same person. Ultimately it was her example as much as her success that was to make such a contribution to the sport of which she was such a respected part.

ACKNOWLEDGMENTS

The publishers and the author wish to thank the following sources for permission to reproduce the photgraphs on the pages specified:

Trimoco, 1, 3, 6, 10, 93, 94, 95, 113, 124, 128; Richard Earle, 2, 54, 71, 104, 105, 106; Mr and Mrs Bradley, 12, 13, 15, 16, 21, 24, 40, 47, 53, 64, 67, 78, 111; Betty Black, 18; Reed Photography, 19, 20; Sport and General, 22, 23; Cyril Diamond, 26, 29, 39; Birmingham Post and Mail, 30; Clive Hiles, 32, 63, 73, 80, 82, 97; Sheila Hughes, 34,77; Michael Drew, 36; Daily Express, 37; Pony/Light Horse Magazine, 43; Jean Bridel, 44; Keystone Press Agency, 48, 50 69, 76, 109; Mandy Barber, 51, 87, 88, 89; Foto-Brauweiller, 55, 57; Derek Rowe, 61; Judy Meakin, 66; Eric Marsh, 85; Bob Langrish, 99; Patrick O'Dwyer, 101; Gordon Jones, 110; Tricentrol, 114, 116, 117, 120

Author's Note

It goes without saying that a book of this sort needs the help of a great number of people — so many, in fact, that to list them all would be an impossibility. However, there are some whose assistance simply cannot go unthanked. Firstly, my heartfelt thanks must go to Tom and Doreen Bradley. Despite the burden of their deep grief, Mr and Mrs Bradley gave freely of their time and relived Caroline's early years for me, even though there was a great deal of pain in the telling. If this tribute is dedicated to anyone it is to them.

I must also thank British *Chef d'Equipe* Ronnie Massarella, who had lost his 'favourite' but still searched his memory for stories; BSJA Press Officer Liz Richards who supplied very useful cuttings; and the BSJA itself for computer printouts of Caroline's career which unfortunately turned out to be too detailed to use. Sally Tooth of Tricentrol and Caroline's unofficial 'agent' Peter Pleasance were also very generous with assistance and advice.

As a mark of respect to Caroline, and in my own small way an attempt to put something back into the sport she loved so much, I have asked the publisher to send a percentage of the royalties from this book to Riding for the Disabled. The Charity was chosen by Mr and Mrs Bradley as one close to Caroline's heart. I only hope it goes some way in keeping the memory of this remarkable young woman alive.

CHAPTER 1

The Very Determined Little Madam

When Doreen Bradley gave birth to her second daughter in April 1946 it would have taken a clairvoyant to predict that a career at the top of show jumping was in prospect. The new baby, Caroline, was born into a comfortably off but by no means wealthy family that was making the best of the rigours and hardships of post-war Britain. Caroline's father, Tom, was a country land agent and valuer with little personal experience of horses but Doreen, who came from farming stock, was a keen huntswoman and brought a hunter with her into the marriage. That particular horse had to go as the frugal times would not allow Tom to carry the expense of a horse for just two days hunting a week. It was a bitter blow for Doreen but she was a practical woman and she knew that times would improve. She also determined that her children would have the benefit of horses in their lives.

But when a horse did come into the little Caroline's life it was not in the form of the sleek, well-groomed and proud jumper that she was to be associated with later. Caroline had a much more modest start.

It all started in the war period when Tom's father was unable to get a petrol allowance. In order to be mobile he bought himself a New Forest pony and a trap and began to use it for day to day transportation. Soon, however, he tired of the feeding and time required to look after the animal and he drove it over to Tom and Doreen who were living in the tiny village of Tyringham near Newport Pagnell. The pony and trap was given as a present to the young family and in Tom's words was — 'the beginning of the downfall of the Bradley family.'

All of this however happened in the year before Caroline was born. That first pony became the love of Judith, Caroline's elder sister, so, as soon as Caroline herself was able to walk, Tom had to find another pony in order to keep peace in the home.

Right from the word go Caroline was horse-mad. There was never any pressure

First prize for the dog the judge would most like to take home with him. June 1952.

on either of the girls to ride. Tom Bradley's view is that the love and affinity for horses was inbred in both his girls from his wife's side of the family. Certainly both of his daughters, and Caroline in particular, had eyes only for horses from the time they could crawl.

After Caroline's first successes, stories appeared in the press that accorded her superhuman abilities where horses were concerned. In Fleet Street, where the truth is always elastic, the show-jumping hacks of the time had the infantile Caroline being given two unbroken young ponies and told to 'get to it'. According to the scribes, young Caroline broke the two ponies herself and carried on inexorably, with nary a falter, to the top.

The truth falls a little short of this fantasy but it is no less impressive.

When it came to the time for Tom to get Caroline a pony of her own he spent a great deal of time looking for a suitable animal. His daughter was fussy with a shrewd eye for quality and the 'just right' animal seemed to be perpetually elusive.

Opposite
Caroline, aged six, and Misty, a pony that taught her 'not to be afraid of a fast, energetic, ride.'

But just when Caroline was beginning to lose heart a farmer friend suggested that Tom buy an unbroken pony. The farmer had experience of breaking ponies himself and he offered his services when a pony was found.

Finding an unbroken pony proved a lot less difficult than finding a suitable 'made' one and soon Tom had bought a 14.2hh Anglo-Arab three-year-old. The farmer broke it — doing, in Tom's words, the 'most marvellous job' — and Caroline, despite a few hairy moments the first time she took it hunting, went on to considerable Pony Club success with her little mount.

This was a time, for Caroline and Judith alike, of 'messing about with ponies'. The two girls, who could both ride before they could walk, took to Pony Clubbing as naturally as inner city children take to street football. There was no horse transport for them, however, in these early days and getting to a Gymkhana, show or event meant waking up with the sparrows and hacking there and back. Like all keen Pony Club girls they did everything themselves. Plaiting, grooming, tack cleaning, mucking out, feeding, bedding down as well as riding was done for love. Never did either of them say 'Oh, I just can't be bothered'. The routine chores, which are responsible for the departure of many children from the Pony Club world, were always enjoyed. If it was to do with horses it had to be wonderful — an attitude that led to all the stable jobs being properly done and, later, to Caroline's willingly accepted, but unbelievably heavy, workload.

Even at age six Caroline was showing signs of an unusual determination. She had an uncanny 'feel' for horses from the very beginning and would spend time getting Judith's pony 'right'. Her mother is convinced Caroline 'knew her way around horses' from the moment she was born. She seemed to understand their shape and movement. She instinctively knew what horses found easy and what was awkward for them.

Even then, despite a girlish precociousness and a natural will to win, she displayed an uncommon patience with her ponies. She also showed remarkable unselfishness for one so young. Caroline took it upon herself, because Judith was not in the same league as a rider, to make sure that her sister's mounts were safe, willing and well schooled. It came out, of course, as a form of bossiness which Judith had to swallow for the sake of peace. Caroline knew what she wanted and how she was going to do it — as Judith says now, 'She was a very determined little madam.'

As the girls grew up in the Pony Club years ponies came and went. Ponies that had done well were sold on, often at some profit, and new ones brought on. The bulk of this work was done by Caroline herself and, in doing it, she laid very sturdy foundations for the practical realities of the professional show-jumper's life. Even as a schoolgirl she experienced a wide range of equine temperaments. Some of her ponies were bold, others timid. Some were headstrong, others bordering on madness, and Caroline soon realized that every animal needed a special programme, tailored for its needs alone, if it was to achieve anything like its true

Opposite
Horses forgotten for an hour or so. Caroline and Judith frolicking at the seaside in 1952

potential. Getting the best from an animal became something of an obsession with her. With unending patience she would school a horse for three hours at a time if she felt it was necessary and she was always prepared to experiment to find out what was most comfortable and what best suited any particular animal.

For an adult professional all this would be unremarkable. These are the things that have to be done if there is to be any chance of securing a reasonable living. It is remarkable, however, that Caroline, at such a young age, should have developed such expertise and maturity. She was a prodigy in the same way that a child who can, with sensitivity, play difficult virtuoso piano pieces is a prodigy. She was also prodigious in her work and she had a prodigious appetite for competition.

The will to win was always strong in Caroline. Whether it was in the show ring, on the hockey pitch or on the tennis court Caroline wanted badly to win. She was always strong and she found sport a joy as well as a challenge but there was nothing quite like the sweet satisfaction of being a winner.

For Caroline, however, winning was a personal experience. She was always a somewhat reserved and private person and she was never given to outward display.

Some journalists over the years have described Caroline as a shy person but this is a little off the mark. A shy person would not have been able to get out under the lights at Wembley before a packed house and produce an immaculate performance — nor would such a person have been able to cope with the ubiquitous reporters and photographers who pester the lives of those at the top.

What those journalists really meant was that Caroline was always more at home in the company of horses than in the company of people. She was never really at home with the public side of show-jumping but, because it was part of her life with horses, she learned to make the most of it.

It has to be remembered too that dedicated work with horses, especially when very young, tends to produce the more private person. As a schoolgirl Caroline would get up every day with the dawn to school and feed her ponies or horses. She invariably came home from school at lunchtime to tend to her animals again and it was a rare evening when she was not still doing something in the yard at nine at night.

During this time there was no help, all the jobs were done herself and there was conversation only with horses. So it is not really surprising that, right up until her tragic death, Caroline was always happier speaking horse than English.

This is not to say however that the adolescent Caroline was totally single-minded about horses. As a schoolgirl at Northampton High School for Girls she developed a real love of hockey and was on the verge of achieving top honours in the sport. If nothing else however Caroline Bradley was a realist. She knew that to be really successful she would have to choose between riding and hockey and, once she had made the decision for the horses, she dropped hockey like a stone.

There were times of course when she temporarily regretted her decision. At the

Opposite
Showing Just Jimmy his trophies. April 1958

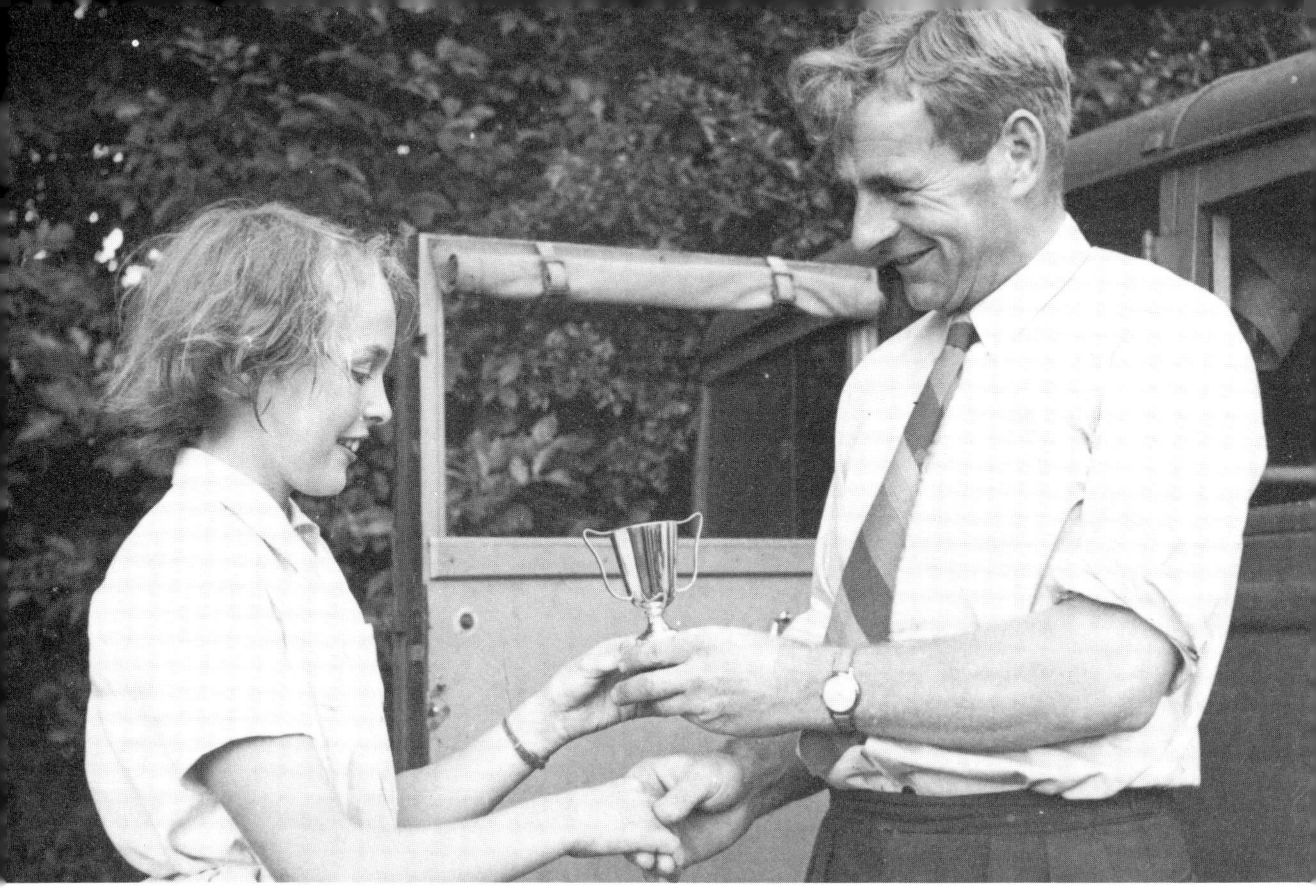

Getting used to winning. One of her trophies at the Newbottle Gymkhana in 1958

World Championships at Aachen in 1978 Caroline had a disastrous (for her) first round of thirteen faults. At dinner that night the other team members ribbed her about it and Caroline, in tears, blurted: 'I never wanted to be a show jumper anyway — I wanted to play hockey.' That statement came from the depths of despair but it was the mark of the girl that she put that bad round behind her and went on to be the driving force for the British assault on the Gold Medal.

Caroline's ability to put first things first was also apparent in her school-work. When it came time to do her 'A' levels she forgot about horses altogether for about three months. During this time the family looked after the horses while Caroline got her head down to her studies. It was not until the last exam was over that Caroline allowed herself to think about her beloved horses again.

During her schooldays the thought of show-jumping for a living had not occurred and Caroline considered for some time becoming a physical education teacher and going to Bedford College. There were places at the College for three students and Caroline was virtually certain to be one because of her involvement in hockey at County level. However she felt that if she took the place she would be keeping somebody else out and she was not able to do this, especially as she could not be sure in her own mind that she wouldn't give it up.

Her father was keen that she did this course because he felt it was important that she had something behind her if she ever tired of 'sitting on horses' all the time.

Caroline however felt it was not fair to keep someone else out when she was not sure and she arrived home one evening and told her father, quite matter of factly, that she had withdrawn.

Tom was saddened by Caroline's unilateral action but he knew his daughter too well to argue the point with her. Instead he took a much more sensible and reasonable course of action. He told her that she could have two years to get horses out of her system. It was like telling Chris Bonington to get mountains out of his system — impossible.

Horses were so deeply rooted in Caroline's body and soul that, as a youngster, she didn't even have time to be mischievous. When pressed the only naughtiness that Doreen Bradley can remember her daughter getting up to was riding her pony, bareback and without a head collar, flat out across a field to see how long she could survive before falling off!

Indeed Caroline's mother is of the view that, if anything, her daughter was too responsible. When there were ponies or horses around there was no idle hand for the Devil to make work for. There was always something that needed doing and, because they always had to make something out of green animals, always something to try to teach the horses.

Indeed the Bradleys as a family are mildly scornful of monied families who put their little darlings on made ponies. Mrs Bradley is convinced that her daughters got more fun — and bruises — from making something from nothing than they would

Even champions once closed their eyes and hoped. Here Caroline prays hard in a Grafton Pony Club hunter trial — the unconcerned pony was called Flicka.

With Just Jimmy at Bletchley in 1959. Just Jimmy had to do everything — Gymkhana, Pony Club, hunter trials and events. He was bought unbroken but with an injured knee. Caroline bathed and looked after the injury and, although the breaker said the horse was not suitable for a young girl, it always went like a lamb for her

have if they hadn't really had to work for their successes.

For Caroline her greatest early success came with her second horse Ivanovitch. In Mrs Bradley's words Ivanovitch was a 'no good Russian'. The horse had came to England with a batch of other Russian horses with the object of racing but Ivanovitch was rejected by its original English owner and was being sold on by a farmer. The Bradley family went to see the horse one foggy Sunday morning when Caroline was fifteen and first impressions were not favourable. Once Caroline had mounted it the horse reared and bucked and cavorted quite dangerously near a stable wall. It was doing all it could to have her off. Not to be beaten, Caroline brought her stick down quite sharply on the horse and it took off. Before the rest of the family knew what had happened the horse and Caroline had disappeared into the woods and the fog. They were gone some time and Mr and Mrs Bradley were beginning to get a little anxious when the errant pair returned. Nothing was said

Out riding with Father and obviously very happy

but, in answer to a quizzical look from Mr Bradley, Caroline gave an almost imperceptible nod of acceptance.

No dealing was done at the time and the family returned home. Two days later the horse dealer telephoned to see if they were still interested in the horse. Mr Bradley had a quick word with Caroline with his hand over the mouthpiece and an offer of £50 was made. This was immediately accepted — with a comment that if the offer had been any lower it wouldn't have been accepted! — and Caroline had her, albeit bright green, horse.

Although that first partnership between Caroline and Ivanovitch looked disastrous to the spectator, Caroline herself was in no doubt about the potential of the horse. Of that first encounter she said — and remember she was only a

Getting ready for inspection

fifteen-year-old schoolgirl making her graduation to full-sized horses — 'I tried him over a small pole balanced across two tins, but even at that stage his neat and subtle jump impressed me.'

Ivanovitch, the £50 Bargain Basement horse that he was, went on, in Caroline's hands, to become an 'A' grade international horse. Indeed it was while she was riding him that Caroline got the first real stroke of luck that set her on her way. She was seen riding the horse by the late Robert Hanson and he was so impressed by what he saw that he offered her the ride on Franco, the 1960 Olympic mount of David Barker.

It wasn't the first time that Mr Hanson had shown a shrewd eye for picking rising riding talent. Much earlier another of his horses, Flanagan, had been put into the hands of a certain Pat Smythe and she rode the horse in the British Bronze Medal winning team at the 1956 Olympics in Stockholm.

Caroline's Pony Club days were with the Oakley and Grafton branches and there were many successes but the promotion to horses — first on sister Judith's 15.2hh mare Nikomis — proved to be a difficult one; at least at first.

As a junior associate member of the British Show Jumping Association Caroline began jumping Nikomis. At first the horse was willing enough but then things began to go awry. Instead of being taken around a course by a sensible and sure-footed pony who went wherever it was pointed with little assistance from the rider, she now had to coax and encourage and aid her mount if she wanted to go clear. Because Caroline didn't have the skills to encourage the horse and give it confidence it took to consistently refusing.

Typically Caroline would not be beaten. She practised incessantly and read every book and magazine advice article she could lay her hands on. Eventually her parents decided it was time for her to have her own horse and, for £165, bought her another mare called Justina. It was a little like giving a boy a broken-down car with no MOT and telling him to go motoring!

Justina was a little bigger than Nikomis but if that was an improvement it was the only one. She was a four-year-old and very green indeed; she was also no oil painting. Justina did however have a very big jump and Caroline worked night and day on schooling her on the flat and building up her stamina. Before long Justina was winning novice classes and doing well at Foxhunter but Caroline made the mistake of falling into the trap that lures everyone who wants to run before they

The Grafton Hunt Pony Club camp at Banbury in 1956. Caroline (fifth from the left) and friends get their tack inspected by riding instructor Life Guards Corporal of Horse Alec Jackson. If the tack was dirty they didn't ride!

Judith keeps the sun off 'star' Caroline before a Pony Club event.

can walk. No sooner had the horse started jumping 'B' grade courses than Caroline pushed her into the top league. Not surprisingly the horse was not ready for this premature promotion and began to stop.

As Caroline said herself: 'In my ignorance I thought she wasn't a completely honest mare. I didn't stop to think that the horse might be getting frightened; I just thought that the horse did the job or it didn't — as simple as that.'

It goes without saying that Caroline did not let herself remain in such ignorance for long. She soon realized that she was making a wealth of mistakes that were beginning to compound themselves: she knew that if she didn't iron out her faults they would develop into bad habits and be almost impossible to cure. It was with this in mind that, one Christmas holiday just before she left school, she went for a week of instruction with the famous teacher Lars Sederholm at Waterstock. For Caroline Waterstock was a watershed.

She took Justina with her and Caroline's first day at Waterstock was a revelation.

She began to realize, for the first time, how complex and subtle an art correct riding really was. Seeing what a different horse Justina became in the expert hands of Lars opened her eyes and, although she knew she had a long way to go, she determined then and there to work at it until she had got it. At Waterstock she was able to ride other horses that were thoroughly schooled and obedient and she realized that she could never really hope to train a horse properly until she herself had been trained.

From that first week at Waterstock Caroline's life was set out before her. As soon as she left school she returned to Lars as a working pupil. For the next eighteen months Lars worked on Caroline and he gave her a very rough time. She was made to ride for hours with her arms behind her back with a stick through them to keep the shoulders back.

Some of Caroline's memories of that period were quite painful:

> I can remember that the first winter at Waterstock was really severe — everything was frozen and the layer of snow had hardened to a sheet of ice — but I was still made to work in the outside manege with people standing around the edge watching. With the wind under her tail Justina set off giving huge bucks. I would fly through the air — still with the stick through my arms — and land in the rhododendron bushes, emerging like a snowman.

In order to straighten her back and deepen her seat Lars gave Caroline daily lessons on the lunge, without reins or stirrups, over a couple of jumps in a circle. Invariably this exercise resulted in the horse continuing in the circle while Caroline went flying straight ahead. Before a week was out she had raw, bleeding knees and ached in every muscle from head to toe.

Never once did she complain or pull out. Caroline was determined to use her time at Waterstock to learn properly and she pushed herself on and on until she herself was satisfied.

In a letter of tribute to *Horse and Hound* after Caroline's death Lars said of her arrival at Waterstock:

> In those early days we had more time available than we necessarily liked. I said to Caroline that we could either go through a few exercises and leave it at that, or go through it thoroughly which would take time with many ups and downs on the way. Her answer was typical — I want to do it properly.

All the groundwork for the riding excellence that she developed later was laid during those eighteen months at Waterstock. As a top international rider she was recognized, by peer and public alike, as one of the most technically correct riders on the circuit. Her hands were always as light as David Broome's — the highest possible compliment and one that cannot be given to many riders — and her horses were invariably collected and on the bit. Caroline would have been the first to say that Lars Sederholm deserved the credit. She once said that if you learn from a master you can, perhaps, become a master yourself but if your teacher is second-rate there is no chance of being any better. There is no doubt that Lars Sederholm was Caroline's master — that she could go on to conquer the world is

as much a tribute to him as to her unflagging dedication, ambition and skill.

Caroline left Waterstock in 1962 and took to the British grade A circuit. The family bought an old caravan to accompany the horsebox and all the Bradleys would troop off to do their bit. Mr Bradley became known affectionately as 'Barrow Boy' for his efforts at the shows with barrow and shovel and Mrs Bradley made sure that the rest of the family was well fed and had as much comfort away from the horses as possible.

As Mr Bradley says now it was a good life with lots of fun and few of the pressures that Caroline was to come up against when she got to the summit of the sport.

But fun though it was, it was also expensive. Some money was made from selling horses that Caroline had brought on and there was a trickle of money coming in from prize money but, by and large, the expense fell squarely on the shoulders of her father. She was lucky in that he never baulked once. His attitude, and Mrs Bradley's too for that matter, was that he got as much enjoyment from it as Caroline did. He loved to see his daughter enjoying her life and doing well and he was always prepared to do whatever he could to help her reach her goals.

This is not to say, however, that Caroline had a silver spoon in her mouth. It is true that she had advantages not enjoyed by most young girls (and boys) striving to make headway in the sport but the Bradley family never had unlimited wealth. The phrase 'what she got she worked for' is true of the whole of Caroline's life. It was talent and application, not wealth, that set her apart from others in the sport. She was a single-minded girl with faith in herself and a healthy conviction that setbacks were only hurdles to overcome.

As she said herself, to get to the top you must work, learn, make sacrifices and never give up. It was a creed she lived by to the letter: a model to all those following in her wake.

Opposite
Out hacking with Judith. The two sisters were very close and Caroline was always ready to give up some time to help her sister with her riding

CHAPTER 2

A Ride for England

All the hard work Caroline had put in, virtually daily since her Pony Club days, came to fruition in 1966 when she made her international debut in Dublin. She took with her Robert Hanson's Franco and her own Ivanovitch and she acquitted herself creditably by winning a couple of classes in her first outing. It was not a shooting-star debut but Caroline was settling in. The following year however Caroline established herself quite firmly on the international circuit. At the ripe old age of twenty-one and on Franco, at fourteen only seven years her junior, she won the Civilian Open Championship at the Toronto Winter Fair in Canada. A few weeks later, also riding Franco, she was just pipped to the post by Harvey Smith in the New York Grand Prix.

The British Show Jumping Association were delighted. Their new young prodigy had brought pride and a touch of the Pat Smythes back to the sport. Several people on the inside began openly naming Caroline as the best British prospect since the 1930s and the vast television audiences began to suspect that a new heroine was in the making.

At the end of June 1967 the British team competed in Warsaw, and Leipzig in East Germany. After the Warsaw competition the Polish Federation named her as the best and most stylish rider at their show (an almost unheard of distinction for one so young) and she became the star of the team. At Leipzig, with Franco jumping out of his skin, Caroline had a double clear, a performance that won her a new riding jacket from the BSJA — the first of many such jackets which were the standard reward for notching up double clears — and she became universally regarded as a mainstay of the British team. Her place in that team was won with results and consistency. It was a tribute to her great form that she kept Marion Coakes (later Marion Mould) and David Broome waiting in the wings; on performance the selectors just couldn't find a place for them in the team.

No sooner had she returned from that triumphant trip to Europe than Caroline

Caroline and Justina (her first horse) take a brush fence at the Fitzwilliam One Day Event in 1962

was brushing aside the competition in Britain. At the Peterborough Show in July she left at the end of the day laden down with a massive Challenge Cup, a gilt Rosebowl, a piece of silverplate and a cheque for £300. On both days of the show she took the main class on Graciano and was head and shoulders clear of the field for the Leading Rider title. An indication of just how dominant Caroline was comes from the fact that, of the twenty-two qualifiers, only four got through to the jump-off on the bone-hard showring and one of the other three was Caroline's second horse Ivanovitch.

Despite her successes Caroline was unimpressed with the forecasts of her greatness. One of her favourite sayings was: 'Lose your head and you lose your seat.' It is a mark of her commonsense and talent that she rarely lost either.

She was, of course, finding that success exacted its dues in the form of unwanted media limelight. Television audiences took her to their hearts and interviews with magazines and newspapers became part of her everyday life. She

Caroline and Ivanovitch get some advice from Mum (glasses) before the Royal International in 1967

recognized that, as a public figure, she had a duty to give something back but it was a part of her life that she tolerated and never came to like. For Caroline the horses were always more important than anything else. It helped her to retain her refreshingly uncomplicated and down-to-earth attitude to life. For her the horses were always the stars and she was just lucky to be associated with them — it was a modesty that delighted the public simply because they could see through it so easily. All those who watched Caroline at work could see that, through talent and hard work, she was making good horses into great horses. She treated them as individuals and worked patiently with each one to bring out its very best.

In an interview with Lynne Edmunds for the *Daily Telegraph* in July 1967 Caroline revealed some of the level-headedness that was rocketing her to the top: 'If I hit a fence in a big competition I just curse and immediately forget it — it's only when I'm jumping with a team that I get worried.'

On her horses she was more specific.

There has to be this instinctive communication between horse and rider otherwise you just can't work together. Franco is a marvellous horse but a bit of an old devil who has to be fooled into doing his best. You just can't boot him in the ribs and say 'jump it'. But my horse Ivanovitch has got a truly Russian temperament. He scares himself when jumping but has terrific character and still has the guts to go on. You just have to help him maintain his confidence.

It sounds all so simple but how do you fool an old horse who knows all the tricks and how do you help a horse who frightens himself into overcoming his own fear? It is in these areas of horsemanship that Caroline really excelled. She could communicate with horses and her love for them encouraged best performances. As one journalist said at the time — 'When a horse sees Caroline Bradley he accepts her immediately as one of his own' — and he didn't mean it unkindly.

Anyone who has horses gets used to disasters. Horses get colds, coughs, colic and depression just like humans and Caroline's horses were no different from the equine hoi-polloi. The difference was that when one of her horses became sick or lame it was Caroline who sat up through the night tending to its needs. In the early days, of course, she had no-one else to do it but even later, as a successful professional with full-time grooms, it was always Caroline herself who burned the midnight oil with a sick animal. Throughout her life the welfare of the horses always came first and, as she preferred the company of horses to people anyway, she found it natural to tend and mother them as she would children: indeed to a large extent they were her children.

Unfortunately for Caroline some of these children had other parents as well. In order to make ends meet, and to finance her exploits in the show ring, Caroline had to teach, take liveries and bring on young horses for other people. Being Caroline, she became attached to all of these animals and, from quite an early stage in her career, had to suffer the agonies of losing a loved horse that she had transformed from nothing into an 'A' grade jumper. It was a little like getting a lump of raw clay from someone, making it into a handsome vase and then having to give it back because somebody else owned the clay.

Strong though she was Caroline was never able to get used to the trauma of losing one of her charges. Even when she was firmly established at the top and accustomed to the realities of wheeling and dealing in horses as an essential part of the international show jumping survival technique, she still felt the loss of a horse deeply. Many an evening was spent in tears with her mother in the kitchen of the family's lovely, rambling, house in the Warwickshire village of Priors Marston because one of the horses was going back home from whence it came. For the owner, of course, the operation made sense. A raw animal was put in at one end, modest livery paid while the schooling was done and a valuable and highly desirable capable jumper was the end result. Naturally many owners wanted to take their profit and start the process all over again — what they didn't know was that little bits of Caroline Bradley went with all of those horses that were sold on.

Of course not all the horses Caroline had in her care were rags to riches stories. Top horses are, after all, just as rare as top-class track athletes. Nevertheless it is true to say that every horse that Caroline had prospered under her tutelage. Those that lacked the special ingredients required for the top invariably became capable

Ivanovitch flying the water at Southampton. When she first got him Ivanovitch had a dread of water but patient work got him to the stage where, even though he was still afraid, he rarely put a foot wrong.

performers at some level of the sport — and all were considerably more valuable after they had been in her hands.

There is an old saying in the horse world, and in the non-horse world too for that matter, that horse dealers make used car dealers look positively honest. By and large this is true. It is somehow considered acceptable, even amongst the most genteel, charming and law-abiding members of the horse-owning community, to lie through the back teeth in order to sell a horse. Some horse owners even feel a certain pride and satisfaction if they have been able to sell on a horse with nevicula or some such disease to a poor, unsuspecting purchaser.

To her great credit Caroline Bradley was never counted among such people. If anything she erred on the side of straight from the shoulder honesty. If she felt a horse was not going to make the grade as a show jumper she would tell the owner so immediately instead of continuing to take income for a horse she knew was beyond even her capabilities. There are many horses in England enjoying nice lives as hunters, team chasers or some such activity. Those horses are happy, their owners are happy and Caroline would certainly be happy that the horses were doing something they enjoyed instead of being bullied into doing something well beyond them.

Naturally it was not such an emotional break for Caroline to part with a horse that was not performing for her in the ring but she was always anxious to see that the horse was allowed to find its own level. She still worried about them.

Being human however it was the loss of the horses that were doing well for her on the circuit that hurt the most and caused those evenings of tears.

One particular horse that Caroline shed a lot of tears over was a grey called Wood Nymph that was being taken from her to go to the Olympics. At the time she had just met John Harding, the owner of Marius, and was shedding a quiet tear over Wood Nymph while Mr Harding was in the room. Wood Nymph was not a wonderful horse but Caroline had been able to get a tune out of it that nobody else had been able to achieve and now it was off to the Olympics, a competition barred to Caroline as a professional.

John Harding was moved by Caroline's tears and promised her that if she clicked with Marius the horse would never be taken away from her. He kept his word. As a horse-lover however Caroline would always have preferred to lose a horse than to see a horse suffer. She really hated to see horses ill and she always suffered with them when they were. One occasion that saddened her particularly occurred in March 1979. On her return to Priors Marston after winning the £9,000 Everest Grand Prix at the National Exhibition Centre, Birmingham, she found two of her horses dead in their boxes from colic. The horses, both young novices, had been taken ill a couple of days before. The vet had been called and, after treatment, both seemed to be responding and taking more interest in their feed. To find them dead after the relief of thinking they were on the mend was shattering for Caroline. A more hard-bitten professional would have been able to take such a loss as part of the job but Caroline was only hard bitten in her love for horses — she took the loss of those two youngsters very hard indeed.

The years following Caroline's international debut in 1966 saw her improving with almost every ride. Ever the perfectionist, she continued doing what she loved best and regularly found herself a member of the Great Britain team. By 1973, on a mare called True Lass that had formerly been with Harvey Smith, she was secure in her place among the élite of the world's top riders, and she underlined that position by finishing as runner-up in the European Championships in Vienna.

A little book called *Who's Who in International Show Jumping* follows its listing of Caroline's second in Vienna by saying 'the same year she turned professional'. What the book should have said was, 'the same year Caroline was *forced* into professionalism'.

Almost more than anything else in the world Caroline wanted to take part in an Olympic Games. She had missed out on the team for 1972 and had set her sights on 1976 only to have the stewards of the British Show Jumping Association destroy all her dreams.

After the 1972 Olympics a special committee of the BSJA had laid down provisions defining the difference between professional and amateur status. Basically the position was that if a rider rode horses belonging to anyone other than immediate family he or she had to be licensed as a professional. There were other considerations of course but in a nutshell that was it.

The provisions of the BSJA were published at the annual general meeting in November 1972 and endorsed by the Duke of Edinburgh, the President of the International Equestrian Federation, at the general assembly in Brussels in December.

Following the FEI endorsement the top riders in Britain were informed by the BSJA of their status: Caroline, along with Ted Edgar and several others, found herself in the professional ranks.

She immediately appealed but a meeting of the BSJA stewards on 7 February 1973 upheld the professional classification and she was told that from that moment on she would have to ride on a professional licence. It was a ridiculous decision and one that angered Caroline considerably. In a statement issued by the stewards they said that, having heard evidence from Caroline and Ted Edgar (the only two riders to contest the professional classification), they regretted that they could not consider the riders eligible for amateur permits. Both Caroline and Ted could have appealed again on the 22nd of the same month but Ted accepted his fate, albeit reluctantly, and Caroline was sick of the business and couldn't see the officials changing their minds.

Apparently the stewards had given both riders a courteous hearing and Ted Edgar told *The Times* afterwards:

The stewards were very fair and did not get me in there just to throw the book at me. They treated me as a friend and they leant my way to try to keep me an amateur — but I am nevertheless very happy with my arrangements. People who haven't approached the stewards, and have just accepted the facts as the gossips around the shows interpreted them, have been very stupid. A lot of them could have got out of it. If their father owns the horses they ride, does the buying and selling and they simply ride for him, they can still stay amateur.

Caroline was told pretty much the same but, unlike Ted Edgar, she was convinced the ruling was petty, stupid and unfair. One of the questions she was asked was, 'Do you do anything else other than ride horses?' Her blunt, but truthful answer of 'No' sealed her unfortunate fate. It was true, she did ride horses for other people — Franco for Robert Hanson and Marius for John Harding being just two examples — but she did not receive payment for doing so. She rode the horses only because the owners wanted to see their horses doing well and because they felt the horses had their best chances of top honours in Caroline's hands.

Opposite
Caroline and sister Judith with True Lass (a former Harvey Smith horse) at the Greater London Horse Show, Clapham Common, 1973.

Caroline with (left to right) Justina, Fancy Trix and Graciano which she rode into first and third in the Wills Young Rider competition at Newport Pagnell, 1966 — her debut year for Britain.

By and large she kept the prize money she won on these horses but without doing that she would have had to charge more for the liveries in her yard. She made her living from teaching, buying and selling and looking after other people's horses; she did not make her living from riding other people's horses — that she did for fun. Unfortunately the BSJA could not see the distinction. To them riding Marius for John Harding made her a professional. They could not see the difference between Mr Harding, a private owner, and a commercial sponsor.

Today the BSJA decision is almost laughable: it was the tunnel-vision of bureaucracy taken to extremes. The late sixties and early seventies were the days when the Olympic movement in general was getting very hot under the collar about 'shamateurism' in sport. They had had a lot of trouble with sponsorship and skiers at the 1968 winter Olympics in Grenoble and attempts, doomed though they were, were being made in all the Olympic sports to get back to the age-old Olympic ideal of amateurs competing only for the glory of sport. In fact, of course, the technological boom in sport, and the resultant expense for any sportsman who wanted to get to the top, had killed off true amateurism years before. Many athletes were getting backhanders from equipment companies and many were full-time professionals in all but name.

But it would have taken a very elastic mind indeed to put Caroline Bradley in this category. Even with the money she was making from her teaching and dealing, she still had to rely on the help of her father to allow her to keep her head above water in a sport with very high costs and very modest winnings.

Opposite
Caroline, carrying reminders of a fall two days earlier at Harwood Hall, with Walky Talky in 1969. She won the Foxhunter Championship on this horse.

When Ted and Caroline lost their appeals in February 1973 they did so as guinea pigs for the rest of the riding fraternity; there were never any other appeals. One of those who did get an amateur permit at that time was Graham Fletcher but 'there are not many of us left' he told *The Times* rather sadly.

Many people within the sport believe that had Caroline appealed again in late 1974 or very early 1975 she would have had her professional status revoked. The BSJA were beginning to realize that it would be wonderful to have a rider of Caroline's class in the Olympic team and, until about February 1975, Caroline's financial position had not changed from that which she had described to the stewards at her initial appeal. The feeling is that the stewards would have eaten humble pie and welcomed her back to the amateur ranks.

But despite the fact that she knew the selectors faced an unenviable task in choosing a team for the Olympics and that her chances of reclassification were high because of it she decided against appealing to the International Federation. The reason was simple: things had changed.

'The British Show Jumping Association made me a professional when I was not — now things have changed,' she told Pamela Macgregor-Morris of *The Times*. 'I can now charge people for riding their horses — and if I did not I could not live.' It was a matter of simple economics. Costs in the sport were rising all the time — remember these were the days of galloping inflation! — and it was becoming a burden just getting horses to shows. Grooms had to be paid, feed and bedding were costing more by the week and vets' bills were rising at a corresponding rate. Although she had held out for longer than she could really afford she now realized that unless she began charging for her services on a professional basis she faced the prospect of having to give up top show-jumping altogether: for Caroline that was unthinkable.

With this tacit acceptance of professionalism Caroline finally gave up all hope of ever representing her country in the Olympics but unfortunately it wasn't the only top award she missed through no fault of her own. Naturally, as a professional, Caroline's financial success in the ring was largely determined by the quality of her mounts and in the middle of 1975 she lost her ride on Acrobat, a young grey gelding of exceptional promise. Caroline had trained Acrobat from the novice classes with immense patience and skill; indeed she had developed the gelding's potential so completely that many knowledgeable watchers of the sport were predicting a brilliant future for the partnership. But bright though the future looked the horse's owner decided to sell it to Sir Hugh Fraser who wanted the horse as a present for his wife. Sadly the loss of Acrobat caused more than heartache for Caroline. In order to jump in the Royal International Horse Show at Wembley in July 1975 horses had themselves to be qualified if the rider had not represented Britain in a team in that current season. Caroline had not. She had notched up a very creditable fourth placing in the Women's World Championships at La Baule with True Lass and Marius but as she was not in an official British team this did not count for anything.

Her paper credentials were enhanced even further by a remarkable victory in the very hotly contested Hamburg Jumping Derby in June 1975. In this she not only

One thing Caroline missed on the show jumping circuit was a good, hard, fast gallop. She took every opportunity to go hunting and in this picture is taking Justina (centre) out for a breath of country air

won convincingly on New Yorker she also took second place with Acrobat.

Both these horses qualified for Wembley but now Acrobat was gone leaving only New Yorker as a top string horse. But there was an irony.

'New Yorker is a brilliant horse outside but it is really a waste of time to jump him indoors as my hope for the Queen Elizabeth Cup,' Caroline told a friend at the time. The horse was not able to come to terms with the bright lights and atmosphere of the indoor arena and Caroline knew better than to take a horse into an environment that he found frightening.

With New Yorker out of the reckoning and Acrobat gone Caroline had no horse that qualified for the International. She had useful horses in her yard but they were not eligible for acceptance under the rules.

As the *Daily Telegraph* said at the time: 'Rules are made to be observed but it is time the British Federation did something to help those riders they guaranteed to support when they obliged them to become professional, simply to cleanse their own consciences for the future.'

It was Catch 22. The Burghers of the sport had decreed her a professional who made her living from the sport, only to put rule hurdles in the way that effectively barred her from making that living.

Early in January the following year Caroline proved conclusively that she was without peer when it came to riding strange horses. At Harwood Hall, Upminster,

Caroline looking glamorous at Pattishall (the family home before Priors Marston) with Titch as a new puppy

she nursed a string of unknown horses to take the Martell Cognac international championship. Caroline won with 3,490 points, a full 350 points clear of Pan American Games silver medal winner Buddy Brown. Her efforts also helped the British team — the other two members were David Broome and Harvey Smith who got 3,050 and 2,800 points respectively — to a decisive win over the Americans.

For this competition Caroline had to ride six unknown horses over as many fences as she could in a time limit of forty seconds. In the centre were big blue and yellow planks with outsize Jokers painted on the wings. Jumping this fence earned 200 points but 200 points were subtracted from the score if it was knocked down. Most of the riders concentrated on the Joker to build big scores but Caroline ignored it completely. This was not from lack of courage on her part — nobody could ever accuse her of that. Rather it was because her highly developed 'feel' for horses made her reluctant to push any of the untried animals into problem situations. Rather than get the horses in a 'bit of a tizz' she plumped for six quiet and stylish rounds. That she was still able to take that title deservedly was testimony to the excellence of her horsemanship. Even then, when it came to riding young or unknown horses she was in a class of her own.

But it wasn't all beer and skittles for Caroline. Like all riders she had her share of falls — British Chef d'Equipe Ronnie Massarella would say more than her fair share — and she had her share of broken bones. At Hickstead in 1976 she started out on

Marius with poise and assurance only to find herself flying through the air and landing with a crashing jar just a few seconds later. Despite the fact that she had broken three ribs Caroline clung desperately to the reins. All young riders are trained to do this from the very earliest Pony Club days but with Marius it was even more important. He was a stallion and Caroline was always aware of the damage the big horse could wreak if he galloped off with full steam up into the mares in the collecting ring.

On one occasion Marius did get away and pranced and plunged over to a group of grazing mares but, although he invited them furiously to come out to play, he never attempted to get up to out-of-school stallionly duties. As stallions go Marius was particularly quiet and Caroline was convinced that the horse was able to switch off from his stud duties as soon as he finished his annual six-month tour of duty with the mares. He was a horse that required little schooling and she was able to compete him within days of coming in out of the field but she could never forget that he was a stallion with a stallion's temperament. At the time Marius was the only stallion jumping on the circuit — most of the riders preferring the quieter nature of geldings — but in Caroline's hands he was always a model of good manners: as she said herself 'a real gentleman'. Now, thanks to John Harding refusing to have Marius gelded, there is a whole troop of Marius progeny coming on and it will not be too long before a son of Marius gets an international winner's rosette.

Typical of hard-working people, Caroline never made a fuss about an accident. Once, even though she had a broken collar bone and broken ribs, she told an inquisitive journalist, 'I am very lucky really, I could easily have been hurt!' It was typical of her practical and sensible attitude to the pitfalls of life. For her all falls were her fault. She never once blamed a horse, her attitude being that the horses were in a totally unnatural environment and that it was her job to coax and encourage them round — if she failed and she came off she would be furious with herself for not giving the horse a proper chance.

Caroline was not immune to making mistakes but they were becoming few and far between; certainly the major blunders that resulted in falls were rarities. From the middle of 1977 Caroline started on the first great 'purple patch' of her career. She began with a very consistent Royal Show that culminated in a good win in the National Championship. Riding Lady Inchcape's Berna, another horse which Caroline had brought on from the novice ranks, she proved to be the only rider who could master Alan Ball's demanding course. All the hours she had put in, in foul weather as well as fair, paid off and the bond of trust she had developed with Berna was rewarded as the combination measured the fences with pin-point accuracy. Several of the more fancied contenders, Harvey Smith and David Broome among them, failed to get through the qualifier and those that did found the rest beyond them. At the end Caroline was clear at the top with six riders sharing second place on four faults.

But Caroline's real triumph of 1977 came at the Horse of the Year Show at Wembley in October. Under the blinding lights of the Empire Pool and against the leading riders of the world Caroline swept all before her.

When she arrived at Wembley for that show and saw the jumps she said that horses 'have to be freaks to want to keep jumping those fences and clearing them'. If the horses were freaks then she had three of them. On the Wednesday evening she won the Leading Showjumper of the Year Championship on Marius, finished joint second on Berna and rode her newcomer Tigre into fourth place. Being Caroline Bradley she refused to thump her own drum over this remarkable success. The horses, she said, 'had been wonderful, hadn't they'? But although Caroline was reluctant to make too much of her triumph David Broome did it for her.

'You would have to go a long way back to find anyone who had done as well in the class and I couldn't be more delighted,' David told reporters in the collecting ring. He was genuinely pleased for his great rival. He knew, as all the riders did, the hard work and dawn to dusk application that Caroline put into her horses and if he was unable to win himself he liked to see the winner's laurel going to Caroline.

He was correct in having to go a long way back to find a performance that came anywhere near Caroline's in sheer glitter. In fact in forty odd years the only performance to better it was recorded by Alan Oliver in 1953 at the old Horse of the Year venue of Haringay. In that year Alan took the first four places plus sixth and seventh: an unbeatable achievement.

Caroline's own comments had nothing to do with the record books, however. 'It was lovely to win on Marius but I was almost as pleased with Tigre because he is only seven and he jumped so well in his first full season of top classes.' Tigre, of course, is a whole story in his own right and a chapter is devoted to him later in the book.

For that Horse of the Year Show Caroline was thirty-one years old — eleven years since she first travelled overseas to Dublin as a member of the British team. Despite those years Caroline still retained the girlish enthusiasm that had carried her through Pony Club and the rigours of winters with Lars Sederholm at Waterstock. As Genevieve Murphy wrote in *The Times* after the show: 'Caroline retains a self-effacing and marvellously enthusiastic dedication. She drives her horse-box herself, deals with all the paper-work (including the dreaded VAT returns) and, while other riders are grabbing a few weeks holiday on exotic beaches, she is schooling young horses through the discomforts of an English winter.'

This description of Caroline would have stood true for any part of her life. To the end she drove her own horse-box — 'it is the only time I really have time to think' — and, despite abhorring every second of it, looked after the paying of bills and tax, arranging show schedules and the day-to-day running of her stables. It is also true that her winters were spent schooling while many of her rivals were relaxing but she did occasionally manage to get away herself and twice travelled to Kenya for a week with friends when things were slack in January — even so they were blue moon affairs and treated as a grabbed moment of pleasure rather than a part of her yearly programme.

Largely this was because her temperament was such that she couldn't bear being away from her horses for too long at a time. It wasn't only that she loved

Proof, if any were needed, that Caroline was the complete horsewoman. Riding Alpaca at Badminton in 1969. Alpaca was owned by Lars Sederholm and Caroline rode him into 16th place

them; she didn't really trust anyone else to look after them properly. Not surprising really when it is considered that she was 'in loco parentis' for other people's horses — horses that had a combined value of more than a quarter of a million pounds.

But although she acted in this way it is doubtful if Caroline ever actually gave a thought to what made her tick. The horses were part of her bloodstream and it was work to get their temperaments right that occupied her, not introspective analysis of her own.

She often said that to get a horse right you had to be able to think like a horse — and as she brought more horses up from Play School to 'A' levels than almost anyone else in Britain she obviously had the knack.

But when she was happily chatting about what wonderful characters her horses had (the only subject on which she could ever be drawn easily) she modestly forgot her own hard work that had given the horses their good manners.

'The good 'A' grade horses will settle in any stable. They are the real professionals and when they're in work they are always looking for something to do. It's amazing how they know exactly what's going on. I can go to the stables at 4 o'clock in the morning and get some of the novices into a horse-box to drive to a show and the Grade 'A' take absolutely no notice. But once they get their own feed a little earlier than usual they know it's their turn,' she said with an obvious delight in the 'cleverness' of her horses. For her it was always a case of the horses having learned their lessons well, never Caroline having taught them well. She was far too reserved — almost to the point of shyness — for self-congratulation. Blowing her own trumpet was something totally impossible for her — like schooling a Clydesdale into a Puissance champion!

After the Horse of the Year Show in 1977 the new Showjumper of the Year knuckled down to a programme that would have made all but the toughest wilt. From the middle of October until the pre-Christmas show at Olympia Caroline and her horses jumped in Palermo, Amsterdam, Vienna, Berlin, Brussels and Bordeaux (only David Broome did more — he took his horses to Teheran and Johannesburg as well!). By any stretch of the imagination that was a lot of driving, a lot of mucking out, a lot of paper work and border hassles, a lot of riding and a lot of worry. But it was her choice. It was how she preferred to earn her living. Through all the joys and the disappointments Caroline rarely had doubts — 'about once a year' — as long as she was with her horses and winning in the Great Show-jumping Circus she was happy; and in the purple patch of 1977 when she stopped knocking on the door and joined the Inner Circle she was happiest of all.

Opposite
At Badminton again with Alpaca. Caroline said it was 'only a sense of preservation' that stopped her climbing up his neck.

CHAPTER 3

The Double Clear Gold

With the Olympics no longer a possibility for her, Caroline's target was a place in the World Championship team for Aachen in 1978; all of her winter preparations over the 1977/78 winter were undertaken with the thought of having her horses ready. As a fierce competitor, selection in that team was all-important to her.

Caroline was a well brought up and nicely bred young lady but she had a will to win that allowed her to compete on level terms with grizzled old characters like Harvey Smith, renamed by the *Daily Express's* James Lawton as Godzilla with Spurs.

At her home in Priors Marston in April 1978, while preparing for a major show at Hickstead, Caroline put it quite bluntly. 'My ambition is to do more than compete — I want to be the best. Even at school I was peeved when I lost a race.'

She was talking at four o'clock in the afternoon, the eleventh hour of her working day, and she had just come in from a rain-swept schooling ring where the total concentration of horse and rider had allowed neither the time to notice the inclemency of the weather.

When she dismounted no groom came rushing up to remove the tack. There were some around but they were doing other jobs and if they were busy it would never occur to Caroline not to do the job, any job, herself.

'If you do something you are bound to do it the best way you can,' she said while undoing the girth. 'What's the point of jogging along? If you're in it you might as well try to be the top.'

This had been her attitude and commitment from the time, as a six-year-old weeny, she had been fighting for wins in Chase-Me-Charlies with the Oakley Pony

Opposite
Parting company with Abracadabra at Buenos Aires in 1971. There was no injury from this fall but Caroline had her share

LINEAS

With Titch and Charlie — two of her closest friends.

Club. Only in moments of total exhaustion did this singleness of purpose ever wane.

Sometimes after a show, it could be in Paris, Palermo or anywhere, instead of jumping directly into bed you have to put the horses straight into the box. Then you have to drive several hundred miles to a ferry so that you can get to Olympia or some such place for a show the following night. At times like that I think, 'How nice it would be to forget all this — how nice to put my feet up and lie in the sun' — I think this regularly, about once a season!

Her commitment to winning and proving herself and her horses in a world dominated by men was the prime motivation in her life but she also felt an obligation to her parents to do well. She always remembered and was grateful for the understanding attitude her father had adopted when she was eighteen. 'When I got to eighteen Daddy was very stern and told me I had to go to teachers' training college or university or something like that and I just groaned. My parents were terrific. They said I could have two years to do something, to make a go of it in the horse world.'

She knew that without this flying start that her parents had given her the Caroline Bradley story would have been completely different and she was always keen to win for them as much as for herself.

For their part Mr and Mrs Bradley are just as happy that they didn't press the academic life onto their daughter. Their pride in Caroline was boundless and as they watched her forge her way to the top they knew that to have made her do anything else in life would have been tantamount to a crime.

Once at the top, however, Caroline had the never-ending problem of staying there. 'I have got to the point now where I have to set myself standards higher than a year or two ago. I have to maintain a level of consistency at the highest level and I cannot allow myself ever to fall below.'

The grace she displayed when she did win major competitions always belied a fierce inner satisfaction — often only revealed by a sparkling elation in her eyes. Quite early in 1978 this tightly reined elation was detectable in Nice when she walked off with the Grand Prix.

Mention that the elation had been noticed, however, and she would have been slightly put out. 'Of course I was terribly pleased. I had been second and third in so many Grand Prix it was nice to win one for a change and get the first prize — you would really have noticed something if I had done something wrong; then there would have been tears of rage.'

But for the impeccable Caroline Bradley of 1978 such tears of rage must have been a long-forgotten phenomenon of the past — only in moments of stress when she felt she had let the team down did the strength of emotion overcome her.

Realism, for the most part though, was the hallmark of Caroline. She knew she was in a sport that was potentially dangerous and she knew there was always a possibility that injury would put her out of the running.

'If I didn't compete,' she told the *Daily Express*, 'I would just be happy amongst the horses. But for now the competition is lovely. It gives a sharp edge, a point, to everything to do with them. If I have an ambition now it is simply to be a winner consistently. David Broome is always the model. He is always the one to beat, always the big threat, I want to be like that.'

David Broome would have been the first to say that she was.

By June 1978 Caroline was approaching the very top of her form — just at the right time for selection for the Aachen World Championship. At the Royal Cornwall Show at Wadebridge she pulled off a hard-fought double on Tigre to hold off David Broome and Fred Welch. Everything seemed to be running in her favour.

Her performance in that show caused Pamela Macgregor-Morris in *The Times* to wax quite lyrical:

> No rider from any nation has been more consistent over the years and failed to win an international title. Now, with a depth of horse-power at present unsurpassed, she is poised to hammer home the undoubted advantage which a string of top class horses can bestow.
>
> The only chink in her armour appears to be one of her greatest assets as a person — complete absence of the sort of self confidence that all but Broome, who is similarly modest, have in such abounding measure. Not only does Caroline not consider herself to be 'the greatest' she would be extremely mortified if anyone else did.

Rivals in the ring but friends at home — Tigre and Berna before the team triumph at Aachen

Pamela recalled that Caroline, when selected to join Ann Moore to jump for the Ladies European title in Vienna in 1971, had said — 'it seems an awful long way to go to jump against Psalm' (Ann Moore's horse). Psalm was on song at the time and Caroline, in her own mind, had lost the struggle before even getting to Vienna.

Seven years later things were very different. The championship was wide open and as good a case, perhaps better, could be made for Caroline as for any man in the field. In depth of horses alone she held a big advantage over all the British men on the shortlist.

Although Caroline was a clear favourite for a place in the team, competition among the riders was very stiff and everyone used the Benson and Hedges Pro-Am Championship at Cardiff Castle in mid-June as a stage to impress the selectors. Caroline was confident of doing well and Tigre appeared in a mood to jump anything but she was pipped on the post by David Broome.

Caroline had seemed to have the Professional title in her grasp: David and Philco were only third in the four-horse jump-off. Knowing this she took Tigre — still an

Opposite
Marius, having just performed well in the Priors Marston manège, returns to the yard with Caroline looking pleased

inexperienced horse by international standards — carefully into the first round aiming for a clear, but the big grey dropped one of his big feet squarely into the water. In the second round Geoff Glazzard put in a stunningly quick round on old Pennwood Forge Mill — a performance that put him into equal second place overall, just a whisker behind David Broome who, typically, had clawed his way to the top after an inauspicious start. It was a bitter disappointment for Caroline but she had got a tremendous response from Tigre throughout the championship and show journalists were adamant that she and David were certainties for Aachen.

This was underlined again in July when Caroline achieved one of her primary ambitions: a win in the Queen Elizabeth II Cup. The year before she had ridden Marius into second place in the Cup but, for 1978, the same combination, with Caroline in irrepressible mood, had little difficulty overcoming their rivals in this *crème de la crème* of Ladies championships.

But the Marius/Bradley partnership very nearly didn't make it to the 1978 competition. After the second place the previous year Marius' owner John Harding had virtually decided to confine the old campaigner to stud duties. But Caroline, worried that Marius would get bored with only the company of the mares every year, talked John Harding into giving the horse a reprieve. The result, of course, could not have been happier and a trip to Aachen for Caroline was now assured.

She was such a clear-cut choice that team manager Ronnie Massarella, one of the selectors, had, for the very first time, picked the team for Aachen six weeks in advance:

> We put a team together that we thought were capable of doing the job — both riderwise and horsewise. Horsewise it could have been said that one or two of the horses were slightly inferior to some other horses around the country but with different riders. We decided, however, to stand by the riders we thought capable of doing the job and I believe that the 1978 world and 1978 European team — Caroline, David Broome, Malcolm Pyrah and Derek Ricketts — was one of the greatest if not the greatest team to ever leave these shores.

For Ronnie the greatness of that team went deeper than just a collection of champion riders.

> "They got on so well together. Every morning they would be up having breakfast together and there was never any suggestion of any bickering. They would all go off together to school their horses and return together at eleven to freshen up and change for the afternoon classes. They were an absolute delight in every way and it was a privilege to be associated with them," Mr Massarella told me in his broad Yorkshire accent. And he added, "...and Caroline Bradley was the best of the lot".

But although Caroline was a favourite with Ronnie Massarella she had more on her mind than the social responsibilities of getting on with the rest of the team and doing well for Britain. As well as the pressure of ordinary competition she also had to carry the extra burden of being a history maker. The 1978 championships were the first to be run under open rules and Caroline was the first British woman to ride

Caroline following Malcolm Pyrah, David Broome and Derek Ricketts at Hickstead in 1979. This was the team that won the 1978 World team gold and the 1979 European gold medals

against the men. She felt the responsibility deeply and was determined not to let anyone down.

In an interview before the championship started she said: 'All I can think of is not letting the team down. But I believe in my horse Tigre and I know that he is ready for these championships. I am also aware that there will be the very best horses and riders in the world here at Aachen, but I wouldn't go unless I thought we had a chance. I shall just do the best I can.'

As it turned out her best was quite a performance; but it was preceded by a disaster on the first day of the individual competition.

The championships began on a Wednesday with a gruelling speed puissance competition and Caroline suffered the ignominy of having three fences down — a total of 13·35 faults. She was shattered. At dinner that night with the rest of the team it was a very sombre Caroline who picked her way through her food but the others, David, Malcolm, Derek and Ronnie Massarella, pulled her leg good-

The Royal International at Wembley. Caroline watches other riders before taking to the ring for the Queen Elizabeth II Cup which she won on Marius

Opposite
Caroline and Tigre look for the next one in front of a large crowd at the 1978 Aachen World Championships

naturedly in a sincere effort to lift her out of herself. It was a difficult job — at one stage Caroline, in a flood of tears, burst out 'I never wanted to be a show-jumper anyway, I wanted to play hockey' — but soon they had her laughing and Caroline stiffened her inner resolve to do well in the team rounds the next day.

As it turned out she took Tigre into that imposing ring at Aachen, with 42,000 people looking on, and pulled off two of the sweetest clear rounds of her life. The first, easing Tigre through, cost an insignificant (at least for the team championship) quarter of a time fault, the second was absolutely faultless. It was a performance that won Britain the team gold medal — the major aim of the team at the championship — and it was a performance that attracted the attention of the world.

But to see the team later anyone would have thought they had done little more than win a novice class at an unaffiliated country show. On the Friday night, in the bar of the Quellenhof Hotel waiting to go to a reception in the casino. Ronnie Massarella and his team had a quiet drink of celebration. They stood by the bar, Caroline in a long dress and the men done up to the nines, and chatted softly between themselves. There was no exuberance and no high spirits, nothing of what one might normally have expected from a brilliant team with the championship won.

In an attempt to jolly things along Ronnie Massarella said: 'So here we are, the winning British team — bloody quiet, aren't we?'

Playing it down but carrying on with the joke, Malcolm Pyrah replied: 'We'd have been more disappointed if we had lost. This is the real one — not the Olympic Games which is a farce — this is the real one; the World Championship.'

What he was saying really was that the lack of high spirits was due to the fact that the enormity of the achievement had not truly sunk in — they had shown that amongst their peers, the other professionals, and in a sport where cut and thrust is second to none, this team of four Britons were the best in the world: and they were the best in the world because of Caroline Bradley — without her double clear Britain would have been out of the running.

As well as guaranteeing the team championship for Britain Caroline came within a whisker of getting into the top four jump-off for the individual world title. By just 0.25 of a fault (that time penalty in the first of her clear rounds in the team event) she missed out on the opportunity to jump in the final stage of the competition when the top four ride not only their own horses but the horses of the others as well. As she was well recognized as without peer in the riding of strange horses she must have had a very good chance of taking the individual title. As it was that quarter of a fault stood in her way and put her into overall fifth place — one place ahead of David Broome.

Despite the disappointment of failing to make the individual jump-off Caroline, and indeed the rest of the team as well, felt she had achieved her goal with the team title. It was the most important title to win and when the championship

Opposite
With Berna at Aachen in 1978. Berna was the number two horse to Tigre at the World Championships.

hinged on the round of David Broome, Caroline, who normally did not suffer from nerves unless actually in the ring herself, could not bear to look and turned her face away. As it was David and Philco had a foot in the water but their four faults was just enough to win.

After it was all over and the champagne was flowing Caroline was taken aside by a reporter and asked: 'Do you realize that you've broken down the last barrier of male chauvinism in show jumping?'

With but the bat of an eyelash and with charming modesty Caroline replied gently, 'Have I?'

1978 continued to be a good year for Caroline — she won the Nice Grand Prix and the Calgary Grand Prix in Canada — and the following year she piloted Tigre to a brilliant win in the French Grand Prix at Longchamps. It was a time when Caroline was riding very high indeed. Tigre was everything she could have expected and the partnership went out as favourites almost every time they entered a ring. Of course they were occasionally pipped but when they were — as for instance when Derek Ricketts and Hydrophane Coldstream did a slightly faster clear round in the 1979 Horse and Hound Cup at the Royal International — it was often only into second place. As a team they had become almost as well known and as inseparable in the public mind as the Queen and the Duke of Edinburgh. Tigre and Caroline Bradley were far and away the public favourites and the roar that went up whenever they entered the ring rivalled anything that had ever been put up for those other popular favourites Harvey Smith, David Broome or Eddie Macken.

The extent of her popularity, however, even surprised Caroline herself. In the 1979 *Daily Express* Sportsman and Sportswoman of the Year awards Caroline joined Sebastian Coe as the public favourite. She had never expected such an award and her natural modesty would not even have allowed her to think about being so honoured. But in London's Savoy Hotel — to the rapturous applause of the country's top sportsmen and women (led enthusiastically by former winner Princess Anne) — Caroline stepped shyly into the limelight to accept the recognition of the public. It overwhelmed her. Just as Seb Coe had won hands down for the men so Caroline was a clear winner among the sportswomen — beating Tessa Sanderson and Sharron Davies with little difficulty.

In that audience legends of the sporting world — Geoff Duke, Stirling Moss, Roger Bannister, Ann Jones, John Conteh to name but a few — paid tribute to a woman who, armed with guts and talent in equal measure, had taken on a male-dominated sport and beaten it. It was a moment of glory that she richly deserved.

Typically Caroline's speech at the ceremony was brief. As Express Newspapers chairman Victor Matthews gave her the silver trophy she admitted, 'I'm trembling — really I just have to thank the horses.'

There can be little doubt that as Caroline was bowing to the homage of an appreciative public she was mentally giving that award to Tigre, Marius, Franco, True Lass, Ivanovitch, Graciano, Justina and all the other horses she had loved on her journey from the Oakley Pony Club to the Savoy Hotel.

As the *Express* commented the day after the awards: 'In the age of the Superstar Sebastian Coe and Caroline Bradley showed us yesterday that it is possible to win big, to explore the very limits of sporting success, without building walls around yourself. They enjoyed much glory yesterday — and they shared it.'

The following June Caroline was further honoured with an MBE in the Queen's Birthday Honours list. For newspaper journalists and the public it was no surprise but for Caroline — just as she had been surprised by the Sportswoman of the Year crown — it was a bolt from the blue. She never had the time, literally, to think about herself or any recognition that she might receive and, when it came, it made her feel proud, but humble and slightly embarrassed.

Caroline never regarded herself as a megastar. Her life was devoted to her horses, their welfare and winning top jumping competitions. She was happy doing what she was doing and she could never really understand why she should be honoured just for doing the things she liked!

CHAPTER 4

Tigre and Tears

During 1978, 1979 and the first half of 1980 Caroline Bradley was at the pinnacle of her career. She had good horses, good owners and she enjoyed the considerable love of the show-jumping public. She had proved herself in her sport and life could not have been better.

But storm clouds were looming.

During those years, despite having several good horses at her yard and despite loving them all, Caroline made no secret of the fact that Tigre was her special love. There was a bond, a magic, between her and the big grey that even the lay public could detect when they watched the partnership jumping to victory on their television screens. Caroline and Tigre were like Flanders and Swann, Morecambe and Wise, Laurel and Hardy — inseparable: without a doubt Caroline and Tigre were the most famous girl and horse act in Britain.

Caroline had first seen Tigre in Holland in 1976 and was quite interested in him. The horse was up for sale and had been offered to, among others, World Champion Gerd Wiltfang and future World Champion Johann Heins. But no-one wanted him. All the European top riders found the horse too difficult. They could not manage him and Wiltfang regarded the horse as untrainable and without a future. The first time Caroline rode the horse she felt pretty much the same. Together the green horse and potential buyer approached a jump only for Tigre to dig his toes in and go through the fence rather than over it. At this time Caroline thought to herself that all the other riders must have been right. But she collected the horse together and had another go. This time Tigre took the jump, not elegantly, but did not make the mistake of the first attempt. As she got to know him Caroline began to realize that the horse had brains. He did not make the same

Opposite

With Seb Coe — Sportsman and Sportswoman of the Year 1979

mistake twice and Caroline's hands, so skilled after the years of patient work with scores of novice horses, encouraged the big horse to respond to her gentle coaxing.

She was convinced that the horse had tremendous potential if it was properly schooled and she returned to England to try to find the £9000 that the owners were asking. Birmingham businessman Donald Bannocks was interested and together he and Caroline flew back to Holland for another look at the horse. After convincing herself, and Mr Bannocks, that her original assessment of Tigre had been correct she put up £3000 herself with Mr Bannocks meeting the other two-thirds and the horse was shipped back to England.

Once at Priors Marston Caroline got down to intensive work with the horse, curbing his extravagances, developing his muscles and tidying up his prodigious jump — and it wasn't long before Tigre was more than justifying Caroline's optimism. The fourth that the young horse managed in Caroline's 1977 Leading Show-jumper of the Year triumph was just a sign of the great things to come.

Mr Bannocks was so impressed with the transformation that Caroline had wrought in the horse that, after the Aachen success, he gave Caroline a full half-share in the horse.

For the next two years Caroline and Tigre went from strength to strength; they became the public favourites and the envy of all the other riders on the circuit but, in June 1980, trouble began. In that month Mr Bannocks decided to put the horse for sale by sealed tender, naming 14 July, the first day of the Royal International, as the closing date.

Throughout the first couple of days at Wembley speculation was rife. Many worried that the horse might be sold abroad and there was widespread sadness that Caroline appeared on the verge of losing her wonderhorse.

Then, on the Wednesday just before the start of the Queen Elizabeth II Cup Caroline's unofficial agent told the press that three tenders had been received — one for £80,000, one for £85,000 and one for £160,000. This last tender was from Mr Bannocks himself and it meant that, by paying Caroline £80,000 for her half share, he became the sole owner of the horse. Caroline, of course, had wanted to do the same herself. She had wanted to buy out Mr Bannocks's share of the horse but she was not in a financial position to do so. She felt too that, in view of Tigre's age, the sort of money being talked of was unrealistic.

Once it was clear who owned the horse the speculation around Wembley began again with increased intensity. What was to become of Tigre? Did Mr Bannocks intend to keep the horse himself or did he have a buyer lined up? Who would ride the horse in future? Caroline knew that she had the ride on the horse for the rest of that Royal International but, beyond that, Mr Bannocks was not prepared to reveal his intentions.

Caroline was absolutely shattered by the prospect of losing Tigre. The horse was easily the best in her yard and the rapport and trust that had developed between

Opposite
Tigre, looking as though he regards winning as his birthright, takes another class at Wembley

Stretching for the Wembley wall — Caroline and Tigre about to four fault.

horse and rider had led to a deep sentimental attachment. It took great courage for her to mount the horse she loved and thought she was about to lose to ride out for the Queen Elizabeth Cup itself. And it speaks volumes for her professionalism and for her understanding of the horse that she went out and won the competition despite stiff opposition from Liz Edgar on Forever and the American riders Melanie Smith and Terry Rudd. That win strengthened the tremendous bond Caroline felt for the horse but, although she was £80,000 richer, she knew there was a real danger of losing him.

For most of those involved in the Tigre dealings it was a business matter pure and simple, but it was known that Caroline was desperately miserable at the prospect of losing the horse and this led to a massive groundswell of sympathy for her from riders and public alike: it was a degree of sympathy that took the business participants in the dealings by surprise.

That she was better off to the tune of £80,000 did not seem to affect this sympathy. Throughout she still retained her image as an honest, hard-working, talented country girl who was having the horse she loved taken away by businessmen. As well as sympathy for her plight, and a natural desire within the sport to keep a successful combination together, Caroline began to attract extra support from those who naturally fall in on the side of the under-dog. Against all the odds she had reached the top and she had done it on Tigre — it led to a nationwide hope that somehow a way could be found for Caroline and her beloved horse to stay together.

Someone however had to transform this tidal wave of sentimentality into practical action; and that someone turned up in the form of Bob Dean, a man who for many years had had a reputation for getting things done in show jumping. But on this occasion Bob had a real problem on his hands.

He arranged a meeting between Mr Bannocks and Caroline (with Bob himself as mediator) for the Friday night of the Show and it turned into a marathon session. For five hours the two sides battled but, in the end, they emerged for Mr Bannocks to say that Caroline could keep the ride on the horse.

The main problem between the two, it was revealed, had been to do with communication. In her yard Caroline looked after more than twenty horses with great diligence and love, she drove her own horse-box and faced all the problems of administration willingly if not with relish. What she didn't do, however, was keep her owners fully informed as to the movements of the horses. Her view was that she was the one closest to the horses and the one best equipped to decide which shows they should go to and when. She felt that this should be her decision alone and that the owners should trust her to make decisions in the best interests of the horses. By and large her owners agreed with her but Mr Bannocks wanted to be kept informed of Tigre's movements and he wanted to be consulted about the show programme for the horse. It was not an unreasonable demand for an owner to make but Caroline was not good at getting on the phone. Because of the nature of show jumping and the ups and downs of a horse's moods and form she had to make on the spot decisions about whether to take a particular horse to a show or not. Very often this decision was taken at the last minute when other horses were in the box waiting to go and Caroline, in her haste, would often leave a horse at home without telling the owner.

She insisted on her right, as the expert, to make these decisions but, at the marathon session with Mr Bannocks, Bob Dean was able to get her to moderate her position slightly. She was made aware that Mr Bannocks did want to know what the horse was doing and did want to have a say in the horse's movements. She was also made aware that if she wanted to keep the ride she would have to meet these conditions.

She knew that she needed to go on winning on Tigre if she was to continue making her living and she knew that she needed wealthy owners like Mr Bannocks if she was to have a chance of riding horses good enough to keep her at the top. Show jumping was getting more and more competitive with every passing year

When Tigre was on song there wasn't a better show-jumper in Britain. Here he gives Caroline a copy-book jump over a big spread at Aachen.

Opposite
Tigre looking keen in the Everest Championship at Wembley 1979.

and horses with any chance were getting more and more expensive, even as novices. Without the owners who bought her riding expertise Caroline would have been grounded and Mr Bannocks, who now owned her top grade A horse outright, was needed more than ever: she knew she had to be realistic.

After the meeting Bob Dean, in his capacity as chairman of British Equestrian Promotions, told newsmen: 'Caroline will retain the ride on Tigre who will remain owned entirely by Donald Bannocks. A new agreement is being drawn up which both accept and which, I believe, will be to their mutual advantage. It will be reviewed in the New Year and Caroline will also be paid the £80,000 as agreed for her half share of Tigre's ownership.'

Mr Bannocks, explaining his huge bid for the horse, said: 'I put in this very high bid to make sure the horse stayed in England. I am delighted Caroline will be continuing to ride Tigre. It would have been a tragedy to break up the partnership and I did not want this to happen if it could possibly be avoided. I have had several very tempting offers during the show this week but I believe Caroline is the best rider for Tigre.'

For her part Caroline said that she was grateful for Mr Bannocks's 'very generous offer.' She said the one thing she wanted was to keep the horse and now she had the 'best of both worlds'.

Although the situation appeared to be sorted out to everyone's satisfaction the worry and the emotional anguish had taken its toll of Caroline. She was a little upset that David Broome, one of the people closest to her on the circuit, had made a bid for the horse (his being the middle bid of £85,000). However it would seem that David's bid was never meant seriously. He did travel up to Priors Marston to try the horse but, according to British Chef d'Equipe Ronnie Massarella, David never really wanted the horse.

'If David had wanted the horse he would have bought it. He had the money from his sponsors — cash would have been no problem. The truth is that, although Tigre suited Caroline perfectly, it was not a horse for David. He was worried that the bid might be misconstrued by Caroline but the reality was that the bid was tactical and made for Caroline's benefit. David knew that the bid would not be sufficient to secure the horse but he also knew that, by having it known he had bid, the winning bid would be forced higher and there would be more for Caroline.'

David Broome had three top horses in his yard at that time but they were all a bit injury-prone and there seems little doubt that he would have liked another animal in Tigre's class. His lowish bid however would seem to bear out Ronnie Massarella's contention that he had decided Tigre was not for him. Even when the bid was in David had told Mr Bannocks quite openly that he would not be interested in the horse for Harris Carpets unless the Tigre/Caroline partnership broke down completely.

But this was only a tiny ingredient in the anguish Caroline experienced during the early Tigre negotiations. She had such a powerful emotional commitment to the

Opposite
Caroline and Tigre at Priors Marston shortly before he was taken away to be sold.

horse that she came out of the Friday evening negotiations completely drained.

Before the meeting she told a reporter from the *Sunday People*: 'Without Tigre I'll be in great trouble. He is very, very special. To find a horse of his ability and consistency could take three years. We have a team at the moment but without Tigre there will be a big hole.'

Her mother Doreen did not mince her words. She told the same reporter, 'Caroline just cannot accept that Tigre is to be sold. She is the one who got all the sore knees and bumps and bruises, not Mr Bannocks. It was just a business deal for him.'

From the moment the decision was made to call tenders for the horse Caroline had many sleepless nights and she was more than a little relieved when she found out she was to keep the ride; but she knew that, without any stake in the horse herself, Tigre could now be taken from her at any time.

Once back at Priors Marston, however, Caroline's basically pragmatic nature took over again. The anguish and trauma of the week before was put aside and her attitude was 'least said soonest forgotten': she and Tigre got back into their stride again.

In the months that followed the pair notched up several more wins and a fourth in a World Cup qualifier in Paris kept her in second place overall behind the Frenchman Frederic Cottier and she was favoured to take the lead after an Olympia qualifier in December. But show jumping is no different to any other sport, the unexpected is always lurking around the next corner. In the Courvoisier Cognac Napoleon Stakes Tigre hit the last but one fence and rocketed Caroline out of the saddle. She hit the ground with a thud that completely silenced the stadium and Tigre cantered over her, trampling her as he went. For several seconds the big crowd thought she had been seriously hurt but after a few moments she staggered to her feet, remounted and jumped the final fences.

That fall was quite a bad one by show-jumping standards but it was typical of Caroline that it never inconvenienced her. Despite being badly bruised and stiff it never occurred to her to withdraw from the competition and she declared for the next day's classes as though nothing had happened.

The big news from that particular show, however, came on the commercial front. Caroline announced that she had signed a sponsorship deal with the oil company Tricentrol. The company was buying an interest in several of Caroline's younger, novice, horses and it was a big victory in Caroline's perpetual battle with the bills that seemed to be coming through her letter box faster than she could pay them.

However the Tricentrol deal was to have unfortunate consequences with Tigre.

News of the contract caused Mr Bannocks to send a trailer to Caroline's yard to take Tigre away.

Caroline was heartbroken and was in tears when the horse was driven away but Mr Bannocks said he was left with no choice. He told *The Times*:

Caroline had signed another contract so I was left with no alternative but to take my horse away. Tomorrow he goes to Mr Louis Solomon at Macklins to be sold. Two people whom I

Tigre, whose stable name was Felix, looking not at all like a cat as he stretches in the Radio Rentals Puissance at Olympia '78.

respect have advised me that the only thing I can do now is to sell. Tigre was not entered for the Lancia final, even though I did not give permission for him to miss it. I hope he stays in this country, but David Broome is no longer interested.

But Caroline took a different view.

The new contract, she said, concerned only her young horses and had no bearing on her relationship with Mr Bannocks. The horse was taken from her yard in February but she said: 'I informed Mr Bannocks about the other contract in early December, long before the news was released. I have to earn a living as well as riding grade A horses. I wanted to keep Tigre because I love him and love riding him — now it's up to me to organize myself so that I have six grade A horses at my disposal.'

But she knew that to put together a string of six top horses would be a labour of Herculean proportions and she was very depressed.

Her shock and sadness at losing Tigre was reflected in the press. Pamela Macgregor-Morris said in *The Times*: 'It seems hard that Miss Bradley, brave, hard-working and utterly straight, should find herself in this unhappy situation. One can only hope that someone will buy Tigre and return him to her.'

Caroline topped the table of World Cup ratings after the European autumn circuit ended at Olympia the previous December but her chance of going on to take the title without Tigre was virtually nil. Throughout the show-jumping world there was widespread hope that Tigre could somehow find his way back to Caroline so that she could attempt to win the World Cup in a year that the final was to take place in England.

But the war of words between Caroline and Mr Bannocks went on and he announced publicly that the affair had disillusioned him and that he had decided to end all his sponsorship in show jumping.

All in all it was the most heart-rending period in Caroline's life. Her hard work and patience had made the horse valuable and that value was responsible for having the horse taken from her.

But, sad though she was, she accepted the situation with grit if not equanimity. After the surprise of getting the horse back the first time she knew she was unlikely to get another break of good luck. 'I have to respect Mr Bannocks's decision to take him away,' she said, 'You can't expect two miracles in a lifetime. I only hope that when I next see him Tigre is well looked after and happy. That's all I care about.'

So ended one of the greatest partnerships in British show jumping. The two had been together for five years and captured virtually every honour in the sport. They had won several Grand Prix, they were members of the World and European title-winning teams, they had won the Queen Elizabeth II Cup and they were the leading money-winners in Europe. All of which makes it even harder to understand why the duo was allowed to dissolve — especially as Mr Bannocks gave up the chance of seeing his horse win the World Cup on home ground.

Although Caroline had accepted in her heart that Tigre was lost, a long-time friend, Trevor Simmons, tried desperately to get the horse back for her. Mr Simmons, a Northamptonshire businessman, raised £100,000 in an attempt to buy Tigre for Caroline. The horse was at the dealer Louis Solomon's yard (it was Mr Solomon who had first brought Tigre to Caroline's attention) and was up for offers but Mr Solomon said he had a firm, though anonymous, bid of £150,000 from America.

Mr Simmons was sceptical. 'I have offered £100,000 and it was welcomed although Mr Solomon says he has had the American offer for sixty hours. Why doesn't he take it? I can't see ourselves going any higher — but that anonymous American bid strikes me as a bit of horse trading and to be taken with a pinch of salt,' he said.

Mr Simmons appealed to anyone who could top the offer to reunite Tigre and Caroline. He said he was unable to go any higher and he called on anyone who could to come forward.

Opposite
Receiving the prize from Princess Margaret after winning the Queen's Cup on Tigre in 1980

'It's heartbreaking,' he said, 'Caroline has worked so hard and done so well with Tigre. He is not an easy horse but she can get the best from him, and to have them parted would be a disaster.'

Unfortunately Caroline's initial pessimism proved to be correct. After weeks of speculation it was announced, in April 1981, that the horse would go to Paddy McMahon as part of a new sponsorship deal.

The dreadful irony is that the horse was never consistently in the top flight again. Without that special magic that allowed Caroline and Tigre to 'click' he became not much more than a run of the mill grade A horse.

There are some, Ronnie Massarella being one, who believe that Caroline had had the best out of Tigre anyway. Ronnie is convinced that Tigre could not have gone on to even greater heights.

'He is a good horse today and he was a good horse when they parted but his peak was when she had him. He wouldn't have gone to greater heights, his great heights were 1978 and 1979. She shouldn't have lost him, he was still a lot better than anything else she had in her yard but he was past his very best and I think Caroline knew that,' Mr Massarella said after Caroline's death.

But whether Tigre was past his best or not Caroline was lost without him. With Tigre in the yard there were no problems. The public came to see him just standing in a meadow and he got his own share of hero worship but, without him, Caroline, as Britain's premier horsewoman, no longer had the calibre of horse in the yard to keep her in the top leagues — and she believed it was all her fault.

In an interview with Michael McDonnell of the *Daily Mail* in March 1981, just a few weeks after Tigre was taken away, Caroline said: 'I'd become complacent. I had a number of outstanding horses and didn't bother too much about bringing on the others. Do you know I once had five horses in one final — four of them in the jump-off — but suddenly all that changed.'

She had made a bad mistake not bringing her younger horses on as fast as she should have, but Caroline, like Tigre, never made the same mistake twice. With Tigre gone she gave all her attention to the youngsters and concentrated on giving her new sponsors Tricentrol, who did not interfere and let her get on with the job in her own way, value for their money. The sadness and the great irony is that she was just beginning to see the results of that programme when she died.

CHAPTER 5

Great Mitts and Mucking Out

The home that Caroline Bradley shared with her parents in the picture postcard Warwickshire village of Priors Marston was where she most liked to be. In this quiet and delightful village, almost the perfect spot for a country girl with a passion for horses, Caroline's father had fashioned a yard of imposing stables for her and altered part of one wing of the family's stately but very homely manor-type house so that Caroline could live separately and run her business without the family always under her feet. It was just as well because her daily schedule had more in common with Victorian workhouses than the generally more relaxed working day of the 1980s.

Caroline's day began at 6.30 — 'not particularly early but as we have to get up much earlier on show days I feel 6.30 is quite early enough for an ordinary day' — and she was always the first into the yard. She would have had a cup of coffee, nothing else, and would set to work immediately putting up the feeds for all the horses. Whenever she was at home Caroline did this herself. The grooms would take the feed buckets to the individual horses but Caroline liked to make sure herself that each horse was getting exactly the feed she had determined it should have.

On all matters pertaining to the horses in the yard she was very particular. She once said: 'Ideally I would like to look after my horses myself as I find it very satisfying. Unfortunately I do not have the time now but I feel it is important that whoever does perform this task should be not only efficient but also have feeling for the horses they do.'

There were always about ten helpers in the Priors Marston yard — five of them full-time — and Caroline was a strict taskmaster although she often felt that the girls got away with too much and that she was too easy with them. She was always aware of the value of her horses — not just in financial terms — and she knew only too well that they did best if given the benefit of a tight and structured routine.

Telling Charlie he had to stay at home. Caroline took him everywhere in Britain but Charlie wasn't allowed to go on the continental trips and he pined non-stop until she returned. Here Caroline is preparing to depart with Franco in 1974.

The girls themselves, as in all stables, whether they be show jumping, racing or private livery yards, were paid a pittance. But there was never a complaint. As one of them said, 'When you have worked here for a year you can get a job anywhere.' That girl was sixteen and had gone to Caroline straight from school without ever having worked with horses before. She knew that she could have no better introduction — it was a bit like a young mechanic getting his first job on a Formula One Grand Prix team.

After feeding the next job on the agenda was mucking out and, again, Caroline 'mucked-in' with the girls. She had very definite ideas about what a good horse bed should be and she made sure that all of her horses had the best.

Opposite
With Marius at home at Priors Marston — the bread and butter work.

Over and over again until you get it right. Caroline schooling one of her youngsters in Warwickshire; work that led to her reputation as one of the best schoolers of young horses in the world.

As well as the essential chores relating to food and bedding the horses all had to be worked, and again Caroline was in the thick of it. If she had had her way she would have had all the horses worked and back in their stalls by ten in the morning but a shortage of work riders made this impossible. Her grade A horses would be worked first because their highly tuned bodies and minds needed the stability of routine and they would be followed by those getting normal schooling or hacking. Her youngest and greenest horses would always be left until last — perhaps the key to Caroline's success. These were the horses that got her special attention. Each had a different need and Caroline worked on each as an individual. She didn't like being restricted in the amount of time she could spend with any one of them. The young ones were really her true loves. They were the raw clay of her craft and she was the best in the business at finding in each of them that special bit of individual talent that each of them had. It is true that sometimes she would send a young horse back to an owner with a message that the horse had nothing going for it but this was a rarity in the Bradley yard. She believed in the horses and she believed that each of them, rather like humans, had something that they could do better than the others. Her record of success with them was ample testimony that she was right.

Lunch was always fed to the horses at 12.45 precisely. As with the morning feed Caroline would make up the buckets herself but once the animals were fed she liked to have the yard empty of people until 2.30 so that the horses could munch away in peace.

As well as being peace for the horses this was also the only break in the day for Caroline herself. She would have her own lunch, often with her family, but more often than not it was a bite and dash affair. There were vets to talk to, farriers to arrange, feed stores to check, show acceptances to organize and bills to pay (and, although not as often as Caroline would have liked, money to bank). She said herself that when the horses were relaxing she like to relax but the truth was that she invariably crammed more work into her lunch than many pack into a day.

After lunch Caroline would very often strap several of the horses herself. In the section on stable management in her own book *Showjumping* she said: 'I find strapping a very satisfactory thing to do myself because I love to see a horse looking really super after I've worked on him.' The quality of her work can be judged from the turnout of her horses whenever they appeared at a show: they were always immaculate.

At a quarter to five time was set aside for tack cleaning and then all the horses were fed again and put to bed with a final visit at 9.30 to make sure blankets were in place and water bowls and feed buckets examined to make sure the horses had eaten up.

Only now, on a good day, could Caroline genuinely relax. She occasionally watched a little television (she liked the lighter situation comedies like *To The Manor Born* rather than anything too deep) and put her feet up. But if a horse was sick — and in a yard of up to thirty horses this was not such an infrequent occurrence — she would be up all night tending it and would still be there making up the feeds the following morning. Even if there wasn't a sick horse there was always the dreaded paperwork!

Add to this day-to-day routine the bread-and-butter work of teaching and there was not a genuinely spare minute to be found in the Bradley day. She moaned about it from time to time but those who knew her well are convinced that even if she could have changed it she wouldn't — it was her life, a life she had chosen herself, and, in her book, a minute spent with horses was a minute well spent.

But it would be wrong to think of Caroline Bradley as some kind of automaton who never came out into the real world of humans. It's true that Caroline was always more of a 'doer' than a talker and her shyness often made her uncomfortable in social situations but she had her friends and she liked to spend time with them; and she particularly liked dinner parties.

Whenever she had one, however, Caroline would make every effort to hide her hands — often by sitting on them. By any standards her hands were huge. They were strong, gnarled, muscular hands — 'not a pretty sight' — and they were

If it had to do with horses Caroline loved it. Here she is hunter trialling with a horse called Romulus in 1966

hands that came with the job.

She often, jokingly, referred to them as her 'great mitts' and would add that they did embarrass her at the dinner table. 'If I take it easy for a couple of weeks then they seem to start to shrink, but not much.'

Although she was often embarrassed by those great hands they were part of the sacrifice she made to do what she most liked doing in the world — riding horses. They were the product of encouraging unwilling horses to do what she wanted them to do and they were the tools that allowed her to get to the top of a sport that was considered tough for men let alone women.

For the last two years of her life, without Tigre, many thought that even those strong hands wouldn't be enough to pull her back up and several people asked if she considered retiring.

Her answer was direct:

If I'm going to ride I want to have something to aim for and there's no aim like the thought of the prize money and the pile of bills it will help make disappear. That's what gets my adrenaline going. Nobody's asked me about retiring before but there's no earthly reason why, providing you take care of yourself, you can't be as athletic at fifty-five as you are at thirty-three.

So okay I've got a bit of a weight problem. I'm nine and a half stone and I'm more comfortable at the eight stone I used to be but that's nothing I can't control.

Besides your idea of me retiring to ride about Warwickshire in elastic sided boots simply isn't on for me. You get more knocks at home than you do on the international circuit anyway.

Those closest to her knew that Caroline retiring was about as likely as Hickstead being turned into a pig farm. She was too busy to even think about retirement — just as she was too busy to think about men.

Every journalist who ever interviewed Caroline asked her about the man in her life. She accepted the inevitability of the questions but they irritated. Her stock replies ranged from 'who would have me?' to 'no, thank you'.

In the early days she went out a few times with Ted Edgar.

'You know,' said Ted, 'I went out with Caroline before I got married but she would not have me. She told me to "hack on".'

Later Ted was reported to have said: 'Caroline is the top in everything: she'll hate me for saying this but she should get a husband. Save her doing all the work.'

But Caroline had other ideas. 'I'm very comfortable as I am. I am sure I am far too awkward and set in my ways now.'

But the real reason for the lack of men in Caroline's life was hit on by her mother Doreen:

It was inevitable. What man would have been prepared to play second fiddle to a horse? Okay I suppose at the lower levels of horse sports it would have been possible but at Caroline's level it would have been out of the question. As well as the horses coming first always there was all the travelling and the discomfort. Caroline got to the top because she was able to cope with it. It would have been asking too much for a man to do so as well.

But there was a feminine side to Caroline. She loved to put on a long dress for dinner and she was a long way from the tweed and leather country stereotype.

'Do you really want to know my idea of luxury?' she once said to an inquisitive country newshound. 'It is to live in a house where even in the winter you can go around with bare arms. At home in Warwickshire we have to muffle up like Eskimos all the time. Even washing one's hair needs true British grit.'

And she would indulge herself too.

'I'd stuff myself with avocado pears, fillet steak, great thick slices of brown bread heavy with butter and then I'd have chocolate cake and a holiday in the warmest country I could find — oh, and masses of honey in my tea and coffee.'

'What's more,' she added, 'I'd buy very expensive shoes, lashings of smelly soaps and bubble bath mixtures. No, not perfume because I win a lot of that.'

It was an uncharacteristic admission of human frailty on Caroline's part but it said a great deal for the commitment Caroline made to the other, more important side of her life. She may have dreamt of bubble baths and chocolate cake extravagancies but she never really allowed them.

When Caroline was not riding horses she was thinking about them. This is a Christmas card she drew for her parents in 1954

In 1980 and 1981 she was able to get away for short holidays in Kenya with a group of friends but they were the only compromises to one hundred per cent effort in over ten years. 'I am sometimes able to relax when things get quiet in January and when I can I like to go somewhere hot. I like to do absolutely nothing far away from horses and just lie in the sun. I am basically a very lazy person.'

It was of course not true. She liked those get-away-from-it-all trips but she liked getting home to her horses even more.

Whenever she was visited at Priors Marston she enjoyed sitting people down in her kitchen-cum-living-room and watching the shock register on the faces of her guests. The first thing to get used to was Caroline herself. On her home patch she was a lot different from the immaculate, well-groomed, first lady of the show ring image that the television portrayed. When she interviewed girls for a job in the yard she liked to sit them on a chair that was always tipping up. It used to break the ice and as groom Mandy Barber said — 'Caroline liked to laugh when others did something silly.'

Comfortable and practically dressed in favourite old checked shirt, old jeans and 'Husky' type jacket, Caroline looked more like one of her working grooms than the Lady of the yard. Her hair, which at shows was always hidden up underneath her riding hat, hung in stringy rats tails, telling only too clearly that she had been working hard until just a few moments before, and her eyes, soft and just slightly watering, had more in common with her faithful old pointer Charlie than a show jumper with the killer instinct.

Opposite
Marius continuing his winning way at Wembley in 1977

The shoe on the other foot. Caroline presents the Harlow BP Sportsman of the Year award to fourteen-year-old Richard Green — the world's third fastest boy over 1500 metres in 1970

She stood rather awkwardly on her feet — almost as though she was unsure what to do with her legs when they were not attempting to squeeze a little extra out of a horse — and her hands, those great hands that chronicled her years of toil, were always in her pocket.

In her kitchen filtered coffee from a coffee-maker was at the ready throughout the day and the general lay-out reflected her view of life. The room was lived in rather than untidy and there were bits of her past scattered everywhere; but not in an ostentatious way.

The few memories of the past that were lying around looked as though they were only there because the cellar was already full. It was a haphazard room. A

Opposite
Unless she was just about to compete Caroline never refused an autograph. It made her a favourite with Pony Club girls the length and breadth of the country

rosette might be seen poking out from a pile of bills on her table, a presentation goblet on a shelf was used to hold a motley collection of pencils and ball-points, a few hand-drawn horse heads on the wall, one clearly marked Ivanovitch — 'he was my first really good horse, a natural, I will always have a soft spot for him' — and the bric-à-brac of the horsey life everywhere, as though dropped rather than placed. The only real evidence of her status in the sport was her rosette board. Her habit was to put up the ones of the current season but as soon as it ended they would be stored away and a new board started.

It was in this room that she was most likely to drop her guard and reveal that the ice-cool winner had the same worries and doubts that any self-employed person might have.

With a glance at the paperwork on her table — mostly bills that she had to pay — she would say, 'I give up nearly every Monday morning. There are two things I really dislike in this world. I don't like bills and I don't like losing. I hate it sometimes, I get absolutely livid when I lose. When you win it's nice, it gives you great satisfaction, especially if that win was on a really good horse, but,' — and she would add this with a scowl — 'there is nothing good that can ever be said for bills.'

The paperwork necessary to keep Caroline's operation going was immense. It was a £400,000 business with high overheads and money going out often considerably faster than it was coming in. Caroline needed to continue experiencing the thrill of being a winner just to keep her head above the financial water. It was always a non-stop worry for her but she insisted on doing it all herself, only asking her father to go over the books on rare occasions.

On one occasion in 1980 she told a riding magazine: 'I frightened myself last week by working out how much it costs to run the yard a week. I didn't go into the office for two days afterwards.' She did return, of course. Her singleness of purpose and her determination to keep on riding never allowed her to forget that the administration side of the business was just as important as the schooling of the youngsters.

Indeed the practicalities of the business had inured her to some of the heartbreak she had felt when she sold a horse in the early days.

'I buy and sell horses,' she answered directly when asked how she made most of her living.

> We get them at two, three, four years old and school them and teach them so that they are five when they first go into the ring. Really cold months can hold us up, last winter delayed us for two months, but the idea is to improve them and sell them at five with winnings behind them. Every horse that actually belongs to me is always for sale at the right price. I usually have seven or eight to sell at any one time.

Sometimes the need to survive in a cut-throat business pushed her even further.

> You must try earning money every way you can. I give lessons and I enjoy them but it's too much of a tie to do all the time. But sometimes you have ulterior motives. You have someone in for lessons because they are very well connected in the horse world — and in the end you may find yourself in the happy position of selling horses just because they have been here.

Time taken out to do some of the dreaded paperwork. Charlie and Titch look just as bored.

The need to make money 'any way she could' led to her celebrated appearance in the Blue Band margarine television commercial.

It was an episode in her career that embarrassed her until the very end.

At first I thought 'no, absolutely no' but then it dawned on me that if I didn't do it somebody else certainly would. It wasn't exactly my line and I was embarrassed at the time — even the kids in this village would shout after me 'there goes Blue Band'.

When the offer came to do the advertisement it was a complete surprise — 'it came out of the blue if you will excuse the pun' — and she was whisked off into a world that, until then, had been little more than a dream or a TV image. She was flown off to America to make the advertisement — 'because there were no leaves left on the trees in England and they said they needed leaves' — and for a few days found herself in the heady spin of the Madison Avenue ad world. Flashy PR execs, producers, make-up artists and the like were all a bit much for the English country lass — especially this one who could talk horse considerably more fluently than she could talk American 'commercialese'.

But there were stories to tell as well.

Above and opposite
Pictures of Caroline Bradley and horses are legion but pictures of Caroline Bradley on holiday are as scarce as hen's teeth. In these two rare pictures Caroline is enjoying the sun and the scrub in Kenya in January 1981

It was very funny because our flying in the show-jumping world is minimal — when we do it is usually in the back with a horse — but this time I was flying first class in a jumbo. I'd never flown in a jumbo before and I never got the time to go to the films so I thought it would be nice to sit back, relax, and watch a film. Do you know what I got? — *International Velvet*! Coming back on another airline there was a film — *International Velvet*! Then I had to go to Australia and, you've guessed it, the film was *International Velvet*.

It's a little sad to think of a real girl who fought a real battle to get from a country Pony Club to the top, being trapped watching Tatum O'Neal playing what Hollywood imagined the 'pony to Grand Prix horse' story to be. The humour of it was not lost on Caroline though.

Embarrassed or not, the Blue Band ad put cash into the business at a time when it was most needed.

It has to be remembered that there was very little money to be made on the show-jumping circuit itself. It's true that some of the sponsors put up very generous prizes in the bigger classes but the competition was always intense and even Caroline could not bank on winning more than a small proportion of it. In addition the reality of the situation was that the big shows were just the icing on the cake for Caroline. Most of her time was spent taking horse-box loads of novice horses to small country shows as part of their overall education. In these classes the prizes were often not more than £10 — an amount that was a drop in the ocean compared with the cost of just getting the horse to the show.

Every year Caroline clocked up thousands upon thousands of miles in her horsebox travelling with the younger horses and the overall expense was astronomical. Even when she had sponsorship from Tricentrol there was no money to burn but in the pre-Tricentrol days every penny had to be watched.

In the late 1970s she had to choose between an indoor school and a new horsebox. She needed an indoor school desperately so that the weather would not hold up the training of the young horses she needed to sell to stay afloat, but she opted for the new horsebox. Using all her savings, she spent £28,000 on a new Ford Turbo, trading in her old box in the process. For someone who travelled as much as Caroline a good box was more important than a good home. She spent a great deal of every year living in it, travelling countless miles over British and European roads with up to seven horses — estimated value up to a quarter of a million pounds — in the back.

It was because of the need to do this travelling as part of her living, and also because she never really trusted anyone else to drive and look after the horses as well as she could, that she took her HGV licence. When she got it she was as proud as she was when she won a Grand Prix class — that licence was money in the bank to her.

As well as being proud of her licence Caroline was also proud of that new box. It had a fridge, hot and cold water and a TV — an important item as there is often a lot of waiting to be done at country shows and not much to do; she had a tendency to be nervous before entering the ring even at the smaller shows (Ronnie Massarella believes that all real champions show this nervousness) and the television helped her to keep moderately calm.

The box offered something a bit more than a spartan life on the road and it was an essential item, but it had to pay its way. To do this Caroline often subsidized her costs by carrying other people's horses. Derek Ricketts lived nearby and quite often his horses shared the journey abroad. At one time she ferried the entire Irish international team across Europe from one show to another. It was nerve-wracking and tiring but it kept her business in the black and allowed her to continue to ride: the most important thing of all.

The box had the other advantage that there were never any hotel bills to pay. It was always parked near to the showgrounds and at the end — sometimes as late as three in the morning — Caroline could throw herself in a bed that was only minutes away and be on hand immediately if there should ever be a crisis or an emergency with the horses.

Despite this advantage it was a hard life, for the girl grooms as much as Caroline.

After final jump-offs the grooms had to wash down, dry and feed the horses — a process that could take more than an hour — but Caroline's main groom Mandy Barber was adamant that she loved it.

'I much prefer it to being at home. You see all the big jumping competitions and you feel very close to your own horses,' she said.

Caroline too enjoyed the gypsy life — she had to in order to go on because it had more than its share of troubles.

CHAPTER 6

Gremlins and Stable Thieves

Anyone who has done any long-distance travelling by car will know that there are times when everything seems to go wrong at once. Punctures, breakdowns, a broken fan-belt on a mountain pass miles from anywhere; once they start there seems to be no end.

Compared with Caroline Bradley's troubles on the road, however, the despair of the average holiday motorist is little more than mild inconvenience.

She faced problems even before she pushed the starter of the horse-box to leave Priors Marston. When horses are being taken on a journey to the Continent it is not possible, much to every British showjumper's annoyance, to bundle the horses into the transporters and go. The paperwork that has to be completed before anything can happen is enough to put off even the keenest aspirant. It is not enough, for instance, for the horse to be registered with the BSJA; they also have to have passports (with photographs and detailed descriptions of markings), travel documents and current vaccination certificates from a vet.

Hours would be spent getting this mountain of paper ready before departure and no matter how much effort she put in 'they all appeared to be deficient in some way when you presented them to customs officers on entering or leaving the country'.

On top of all this she had to make sure that the lorry was properly serviced and fit for a lengthy trip (sometimes a European venture lasted up to a month). As the horse box was also to be a home the living area had to be provisioned and the truck documents and insurances, for horses and vehicles, had to be checked. In addition Caroline had to make sure that she had sent off all the entry forms for the shows she wanted to attend. Show officials are very strict about such matters, as they are even at tiny unaffiliated shows at home, and no entry meant no start. Like the paper work over money matters, Caroline tended to put off getting her entry applications away until the last minute — her personality in this area making her

The kitchen/living room of the new horsebox after the Tricentrol deal. Caroline had never had it so good

the opposite of the ordered and organized and unflustered person she became in the show ring itself — and many times letters came back telling her not to bother as all the classes were full. The shows that she really wanted to go to, however, somehow got the entries sent off with a day or two to spare but it was always a pretty close thing.

It is not surprising really that some of the things that had to be done got forgotten — there were so many of them. Being a one-woman business she had to do all this herself — not for her the luxury of a manager and secretary who did all the work for her — and her natural inclinations were to make sure the horses were all right first.

Just making the arrangements for them was a gigantic task in itself. Horses on the move need their feed, hay and bedding taken along too. Care had to be taken to ensure that the horses on special diets — Tigre and Marius were always on such diets — were catered for and that there was enough of everything for the journey — even allowing for emergencies.

The new Tricentrol horse-box, the most comfortable Caroline had ever had. Her old box is in the background

Sometimes seven horses left Priors Marston for a trip abroad but twenty or more would be left behind. Caroline was always conscious that all the horses were her personal responsibility and she had to assure herself that the arrangements made for the horses staying behind were adequate. She went to great lengths to make these arrangements but she never really trusted them and, if there was a gap of two or three days between shows while she was in Europe, she couldn't resist leaving the top horses in the hands of their capable grooms and flying home to check that everything was running smoothly. These were always flying visits, literally. A whirlwind check of the stables and a few instructions to the girls and then off again to get back in time to ride her horses in for the shows. Schedules were always tight and it was a wonder that the worry of it all didn't result in ulcers: in a weaker person it almost certainly would have.

The hectic pre-travel arrangements over, that huge juggernaut of a horse-box would roll out of Warwickshire — tiny Caroline at the wheel — and probably for the first time in days she would allow herself a little smile. She drove the box herself primarily because she didn't trust anyone else but she also drove it because she really enjoyed it. She often told her father, who would have liked to see her take on less of the load herself, that the time spent driving the box was the only time when she had time to think; when she could immerse herself in private thoughts and dreams. It's a curious truth that no-one who knew Caroline had really any idea what these hopes and dreams were — she always kept that side of her life absolutely private and if anyone was ever allowed to venture in there with her they have never said.

Whatever it was though that went through her mind, the time spent driving the box was when it was allowed to happen and it was a precious time for Caroline. It was also exciting. She never lost the feeling of adventure; the feeling that she was going off to do battle and take on the world. To Caroline those trips to Europe were always crusades.

Any euphoria that she felt rolling through the Warwickshire lanes was often quickly dispelled when she got to the port of departure. Even if all the papers were in order and the traffic delays were slight, the weather often held up a big 'halt' sign in front of her. On one occasion she was in Liverpool with a box full of young

As well as cash the Tricentrol sponsorship meant new livery for horses, grooms and rider. A display of the new gear at Priors Marston

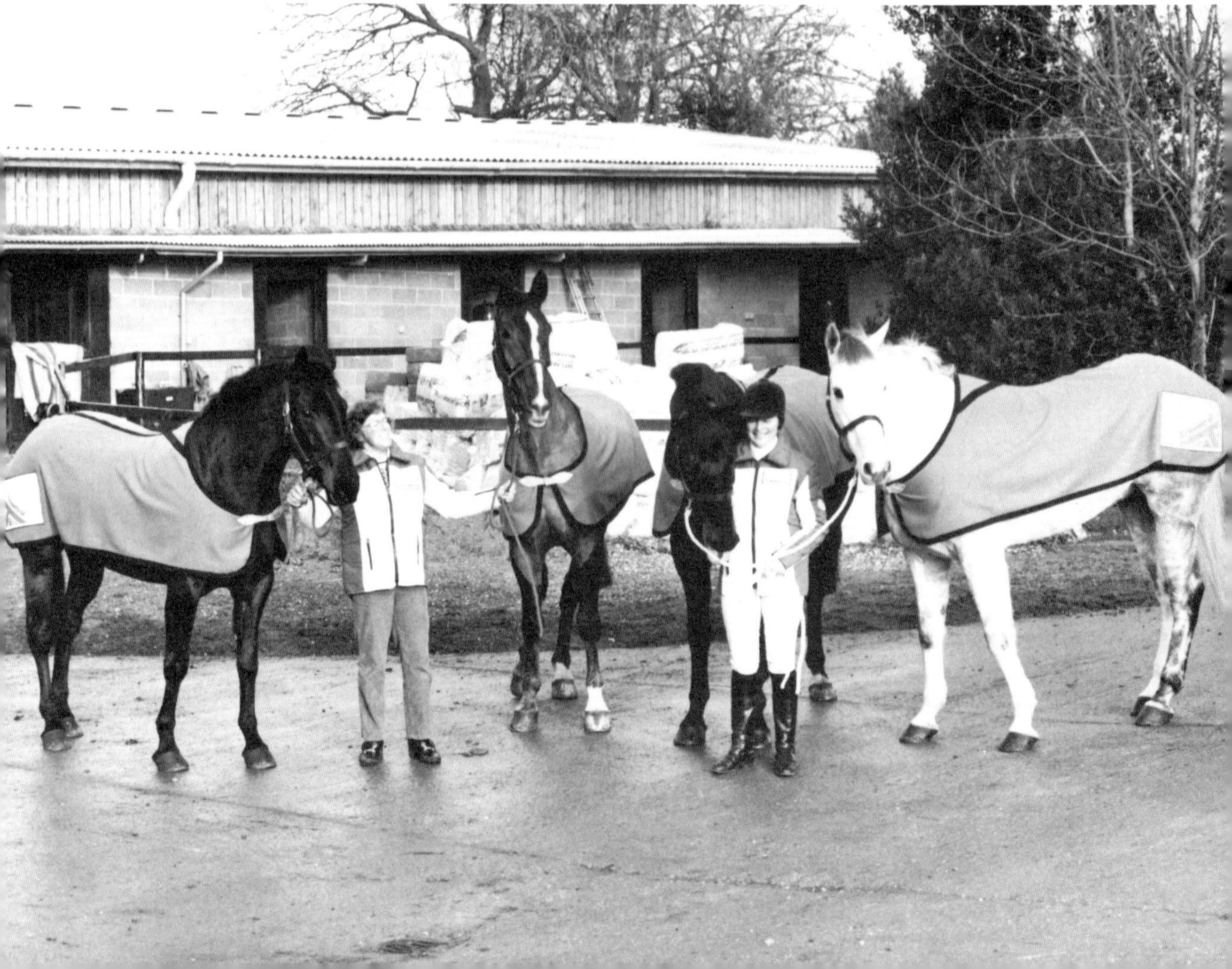

horses stuck fast because very high seas had kept the ferries in port. Her two main horses Tigre and Marius were already in Dublin waiting for her and she was getting more and more desperate as the hours passed and there was no sign of a break in the weather. It was particularly frustrating for Caroline because on that particular occasion great efforts had been made to get the horses to Ireland as cheaply as possible. Arrangements had been made with two other riders to get the horses from an English show to one in Ireland two days later and the agreement was that the horses who were only competing in Dublin — Tigre and Marius included — would go in another box three days in advance. Caroline would then take her horse Landmine and six others belonging to the other riders when the show in England was over.

When a box full of horses is stuck on a quayside it is not possible to leave the horses inside and wait until things improve. Once Caroline realized that it was going to be a long wait she had to rush about shouting her tale of woe to anyone who would listen. Sheds or anything else that might be suitable had to be found for the horses overnight (the lorry had to be mucked out and freshened up no matter where it was) and Caroline had to organize her valuable load as best she could. The following morning nothing had improved and Caroline was miserable. It was all so stupid. There she was in Liverpool with other people's horses while hers were fighting fit and ready to jump in Dublin.

She was just beginning to give up hope when fellow show jumper John Whittaker and his wife, who were also waiting, offered to look after the box load of stranded horses while Carolone arranged a lift to the airport and a quick flight to Dublin.

It was touch and go and it depended on the goodwill of a rival but she made it and Marius and Tigre got their rounds — one victory to Caroline.

Another time she was driving five horses up the Edgware Road in busy London when one of the horses twisted and wedged itself. The frightened horse conveyed its fear to the others and there was pandemonium in the back. Cool as a cucumber Caroline stopped the lorry, got all of the horses out, with a policeman directing the traffic around her, and sorted out the problem. After reliving the story some years later she added: 'Couldn't do it today of course. With the horses I've got now they would run off in all directions.' Be that as it may, the certainty is that if it had happened with her more spirited animals she would have tried the same thing again. She had too much love and concern for her equine passengers to keep going when things were less a hundred per cent in the back.

Horse-box stories, of course, for any horse owner, are legion. Everyone has a store of hair-raising horror stories of road disasters and mischievous, not to say evil, horsey goings-on in the back. Needless to say Caroline had more than her share but it was the ones that happened in foreign parts that caused the most despair and had her pulling her hair out.

Whenever she went abroad she expected something to go wrong and it invariably did. Sometimes it was just a freezing night spent on a desolate wharf, sometimes just a fractious Customs officer, but more often than not it was something far more disastrous and far less predictable. It was a rare trip indeed

Showing how it should be done. With Tigre at Wembley in 1979.

when nothing untoward happened — Caroline could recall easily the bad ones but easy ones that went without a hitch were impossible for her to remember.

Caroline came face to face with the horrors that can be found on a European trip quite early in her career. Long before she enjoyed the benefits of a top-class box she embarked on a trip to Rome in convoy with David Broome's box and Alan Oliver's box (driven by staff drivers with David and Alan to follow later). In these early days Caroline was not up to paying the full complement of professional grooms and she took her mother along both as an extra pair of hands and for company. It was just as well.

David Broome's box was the newest and the fastest and it took the lead with Alan Oliver's in the middle and Caroline bringing up the rear. It was the opposite of the way things should have been. She had Franco and Graciano in the back — two horses that fortunately travelled very well — so, despite the fact that her box was ancient compared with the Broome palace, she was able to keep up quite well. Until they were approaching Milan that is.

It was night and dark — cloud blocked out the moon — and Caroline concentrated on keeping the tail-lights of David's lorry clearly in sight. Suddenly however those lights were gone. Lost into the night.

The driver who was showing the way had disappeared — that was bad enough — but, even worse, he had taken all the travel documents with him; including the whereabouts of the sleeping quarters for the horses that night. Alan's driver to be on the safe side had scribbled the address on a scrap of paper but, even though everything was pulled out of the box, every pocket searched and every hay net investigated, it refused to come to light. They were lost.

After an emergency conference in the middle of the road it was decided that there was no alternative but to drive on to the nearest police station and throw themselves on the mercy of the Italian police: an action considered by those in the know little short of suicide, even if things had only been marginally wrong.

With virtually non-existent Italian this sorry little band of British show jumpers tried, with the help of frantic sign language, to explain to the police that they badly needed beds for the horses. It was hopeless. The policemen, who at first were amused and interested by this raggle-taggle intrusion into their humdrum lives, soon lost interest when it became apparent that the communication level between drivers and themselves was zero. In desperation both lorries took off again into the night with Caroline and the Oliver driver steering by the seat of their pants. They knew, however, that it was pointless going on forever — especially as they had no idea which direction they were going — so they decided to stop as soon as they saw a likely bit of grass on which the horses could graze.

Before long the headlights picked out a patch of green and both trucks hove to. The horses were all let out to stretch their legs and munch a little grass and the lorries were cleaned out with neat little piles of manure and straw stacked up behind each box.

The only fortunate thing on this night of disaster was that both boxes were carrying only two horses. This meant that there was plenty of room inside and the horses could be put back as soon as the insides were clean and they had overcome their travel stiffness on the grass.

By the time all this was done it was very late when the Oliver team and Mrs and Miss Bradley finally settled into their sleeping bags for the night, dog tired.

The second stroke of good luck had to do with Caroline's biorhythms. After years of getting up with the sparrows she woke automatically as soon as the first rays of the sun spilled over the horizon. She called out to wake her mother and the people in the other box and jumped out to release the horses, clean out the box and give them their breakfast.

No sooner had her feet left the box in the jump to the ground than she knew the extent of her error. What she had thought was a field of good country grass turned out to be a field in front of a very imposing and obviously very important Cathedral. On this grass, sacrilegiously parked and surrounded by piles of manure, were two English horse-boxes, four horses and four very startled people.

Panic immediately set in. Without a word bits and pieces of equipment were thrown back inside, ramps were closed and both boxes were back on the road within minutes. Neither had ever got themselves away from anywhere quite so fast. What the Cathedral staff and priests said when they discovered the neat souvenirs of the visit was never revealed!

Being a stallion Marius was often a handful — Caroline tries to ride off some of his high spirits before a show on the continent and Marius shows why his stable name was Dennis the Menace.

They had got away without being incarcerated in some deep and forgotten crypt but all was not over. They still didn't know where they were or where they were going.

On the approach to Milan proper Caroline took a side route off a motorway and realized she had made a mistake as soon as she had made the turn. Meanwhile the Oliver box sailed along happy and oblivious.

Caroline knew that if she went on along the turn-off she would become hopelessly lost so she attempted to reverse back to the motorway up the one-way exit road. Italians, with the expected Latin performance of loud horns and yelled obscenities, weaved their way around the box but Caroline was not to be deterred and continued, slowly and carefully, to reverse. When she was about a hundred metres from the motorway itself the Oliver box came down the same exit road. The Oliver driver, realizing what had happened, had turned back to find Caroline's stricken transport.

Now there were two British horse-boxes reversing, illegally, up the narrow exit to get back on the motorway. The cursing from the Italian motorists increased and the resolve of the plucky Brits was stiffened.

Eventually, of course, they found their way back on to the main route and, with the help of some locals who had a little English, found their way to the show-grounds. Needless to say some very harsh words were exchanged with the driver of David Broome's transporter (despite her good breeding and impeccable manners she was able to make the air blue when the spirit moved her). It was a good introduction to life on the Euro-road.

But it was not the end of her troubles on that particular journey. The Broome driver, despite having received the sharp end of Caroline's tongue, regularly forgot that the two lorries in his wake were older and slower than his. More times than she cared to remember the twin red eyes of the Broome tail winked out leaving her high and dry and lost.

It was still winter-time and many of the roads they had to cross were steep mountain passes. Visibility was often bad with frequent snow storms and for much of the time Caroline's only contact with the real world was the comforting glow of those lights in front: when they were there!

On one such occasion she was climbing quite a steep incline somewhere near Geneva when she saw the vague outline of a hut through the driving snow. Both of the other lorries roared past but when Caroline got to the top of the hill she and her mother were confronted with a border guard pointing an automatic weapon straight at them.

Apparently the other two trucks had not known of the border post and charged straight through but the guards, alerted by the thunder of the first two, had time to organize themselves by the time Caroline arrived at the barrier.

They were like hornets from a disturbed nest. Their authority had been snubbed and they were determined that this truck that they had caught was going to pay the full penalty.

Again spleens were vented from both sides and, again, neither side understood what the other was saying. After an hour or so, in exasperation, the border guards let the horse-box through and Caroline caught up the other two who were waiting a few miles ahead. Caroline and her mother were livid but the others thought it was a great joke. They were not the least sorry and were in fits of laughter all the way to that night's stabling. Later, of course, the two Bradleys saw the funny side of it all but the experience of looking down the muzzle of a loaded automatic weapon took some time to overcome.

Sometimes the international circuit required Caroline to travel to Berlin down the infamous Berlin Corridor: a place where all the show jumpers prayed they didn't break down. Everyone who has driven to Berlin will know what a strange and frightening place that corridor through East Germany can be. It is barren and still and there is an almost total absence of life — there are no twittering songbirds in

Opposite
Backstage with Fieldmaster at Dublin Indoor International 1978. This photograph was taken by Patrick — one of her most loyal fans — and was sent to her with 'love and best wishes'

the few trees that have been left along that desolate road. It is a place where no-one in his right mind wants to get stuck but Caroline, in a run of bad luck that would have had casino managers rubbing their hands in glee, managed it.

There was a rule among British riders that travel down the Corridor was always done in convoy. Everyone felt the spookiness of the place (only the horses seemed unconcerned) and it was felt that there was safety in numbers. On this particular journey out of Berlin, however, Caroline got left behind the other two lorries in the lanes before the border into East Germany. Her lane was slower than the others and by the time she cleared the formalities she was a good way behind. Concerned that she might lose her companions, Caroline put her foot down in an attempt to catch up but she was in her rather ancient box and the shake up on the rough roads upset the engine and it rebelled. The motor began to make an ominous groaning noise and she lost most of her power. Immediately Caroline began flashing her lights and blasting her horn in an attempt to alert the other drivers to her problem but it was no good and the reality dawned that she was in East Germany with six valuable horses and a broken-down lorry; a nightmare in anybody's book.

The only hope she had lay in the fact that she knew that old lorry pretty well and experience told her that the most likely cause of the trouble was dirt in the fuel line. But though she knew her lorry she was no mechanic and began to sink into deep depression as she froze in the bleak East German winter morning air.

Out of the blue, however, came Guardian Angels in the form of a British Military Police Patrol. The British lads hopped out and with a bit of home handyman tinkering got the old truck into life, albeit with a terminal case of asthma. The M.P.s also radioed for a breakdown truck but as it was to come from the opposite direction Caroline decided to continue on ten per cent power until she met up with it.

Most motorists get annoyed when they are following a big lorry at the best of times but when they are following a monstrously large horse transporter doing about eight miles an hour in the single lane of an autobahn they get more than usually peeved: horns honked and drivers yelled as a rapidly growing tail-back developed behind the lorry.

Under such circumstances it would have been a miracle if she hadn't been stopped by the East German police and on that day miracles were out of stock. A car load of the armed and officious police pulled her over and checked her papers while Caroline tried to explain in schoolgirl German what was wrong.

When the extent of her problem was revealed one of the Germans produced a fuel filter from the police car and fitted it to the truck. They were all smiles as they gestured for her to climb in and start up but, although the lorry started, it only moved a few yards before wheezing to a stop. The Germans had had enough by this time and they piled back into their car and took off but the British patrol passed again with the news that the breakdown truck would be about an hour and a half. This was in the late morning and when the help had not arrived by half past one desperation began to set in again.

One of the strengths of Caroline's personality was that she was never prepared to give in to panic. She decided that the breakdown truck was unlikely to come at all and that it was up to her to sort the problem out herself. Out came the driver's seat and, sleeves rolled up, she did what she could with the faulty petrol line. Eventually she had the truck spluttering along and there had been about twenty miles covered before another party of East German police — this time the type that appeared to have had their smiles and sense of humour surgically removed at birth — stopped her. Orders were barked and travel documents, including passports, were removed. It caused hysteria. Caroline had a couple of girl grooms with her who had been looking after the horses in the back during the drama but seeing their passports walking off with a band of East German policemen convinced them that they were doomed to spend the rest of their lives behind the Iron Curtain.

However Lady Luck had woken up after her lunch-time nap and within half an hour the police returned the papers and passports and allowed the lorry, which was now sinking fast, to cough its way on.

Another British Army patrol turned up within an hour and it was discovered that the breakdown truck had been misdirected and had returned to base. It finally arrived at 10 o'clock at night — some fourteen hours after the initial breakdown — and the fuel pipe was efficiently blown out, allowing a very sorry group of English horsewomen to arrive in West Germany at one o'clock in the morning.

The horses survived that incident without turning a hair. They had, thanks to the girls, been watered and fed as normal and they had been given extra blankets to cope with the bitter cold. But Caroline herself found the ghastly affair nerve-wracking and traumatic. It was one of those times when she really thought to herself that perhaps riding show-jumpers around Europe just wasn't worth it. She determined to learn more about engines and she determined never again to put herself at the mercy of men drivers (the two other horse boxes that had left her floundering in the rear as they left West Berlin had both been driven by men!).

Indeed men were often the bane of Caroline's life as she followed the circus around Europe. With much greater regularity than Caroline cared for she would arrive at a show where she had reserved stables for her horses only to find that someone else — usually a man! — had taken them over. Such incidents caused Caroline to fight for her rights with the fury that only the righteous can summon. Sometimes it worked, sometimes it didn't. One time all her ranting and raving achieved was some space in some empty sheep shed — 'I had to keep the horse in with some wire I found lying around but I found out the next day it was part of the public address system, I wasn't too popular' — and she left that show after giving everyone full warning that anyone who pinched her stalls at the next show would be in for it.

Sure enough she arrived at the next showgrounds at three o'clock in the morning only to find Harvey Smith's box where hers should have been and his horses comfortably in residence in her stables. It was a very angry Caroline who pulled the

Following two pages
The Derby Bank at Hickstead. Marius (1976) takes it like a trouper but True Lass two years later doesn't find it so easy and Caroline struggles

LAM

There may not be any money at stake but the competition is just as keen — beating Harvey Smith in the Olympia donkey sulky race is just as important as in the top class later in the evening.

Smith girl groom out of bed to re-arrange the horses; and it was done then and there, despite the earliness of the hour.

On another occasion at Hickstead she arrived to again find her stables occupied. This time the culprits blustered it out by saying that hers were more convenient and that the ones they had been allotted were flooded — 'anyway we didn't expect you here just yet'. They graciously offered Caroline the flooded quarters but it was like a red rag to a bull. She had those squatters out of those stables before they could say Douglas Bunn: nobody fought for long with Caroline once her blood was up.

Stabling was a problem everywhere on the circuit, and especially in Europe. In some places the horses had to live in large sheds with just strands of wire to tie them in. At other shows the stalls had to be put together by the riders if the horses were to have anywhere suitable to sleep. When she became a little longer in the tooth and understood the grim realities of life on the road she carried sheets of chip-board and other bits and pieces that could be used to fashion suitable and private accommodation for her horses. Her concern was always for the horses and she always dreaded the prospect of one of them getting caught up in a tangle of wires and ropes and doing itself a serious injury. If she could she would make the stables more secure by pushing something heavy against the makeshift door so that the horse found it more difficult to get out but on many occasions there was nothing that could be done and one of the girls (or Caroline herself) had to sleep outside the stables to be on hand in the event of trouble.

The show-going public and the millions of television watchers could never even begin to imagine this behind the scenes side to Caroline's life. All they saw was a spotlessly turned out girl and her horses, working together as though they had been born together. It never occurred to them that Caroline may have arrived at the showground only an hour or so before after being held up by customs, weather or puncture. It never occurred to them that she may have thrown on her riding clothes to make it into the ring in the nick of time. It wasn't always like this of course but it happened more often than every blue moon and it was full marks to Caroline's skill, poise and presence of mind that nobody ever knew: she would have been mortified if they had.

CHAPTER 7

The Last Great Effort

In the words of her father, after Caroline lost Tigre she went from being a hard-worker into being a workaholic. The quest for a new Tigre dominated her life and she drove herself non-stop. She knew that if such a horse was to be found it would be a youngster that developed in her hands and she knew this would take a great deal of slow and patient work.

At this time all her horses, with the exception of John Harding's Marius and Landmine, who was owned by the North Herts Equitation Centre, were part of the Tricentrol deal and all carried the Tricentrol (later to become Trimoco) prefix.

Caroline was always happy with this arrangement and she never once regretted her involvement with the oil company. As far as they were concerned she was the expert and they left her to get on with it. They never interfered with any decision she made about the horses and they were always happy with the return Caroline was giving them on their investment.

Sally Tooth, who worked closely with Caroline during the eighteen months or so that the sponsorship was with the commercial division of Tricentrol, was full of praise for the effort that Caroline put in to give the company value for money.

'She was a super person and she would do literally anything we asked her to do. She would always say yes — 'providing you are there to remind me'. Her first thoughts were always with the horses and she did tend to forget things on the PR side — meeting people, signing books, that kind of thing — but whenever we reminded her she was there like a shot.'

As well as giving her sponsors as much as she could at the shows, where the company often had a hospitality box and lots of VIPs who wanted to meet her, Caroline also did all she could for them in her 'spare' time.

Opposite
Caroline and Titch in the yard at Priors Marston.

OTTONS
15

Not the most flattering picture of a Bird of Paradise. Fun and games at the Christmas Olympia of 1982

Opposite
The strain is beginning to show. Caroline grabs a cat-nap between classes at the New Forest Show in August 1982

Sally Tooth remembered one such occasion. 'It was a super thing really. She did a charity demonstration that we arranged for Riding for the Disabled and, although it was outside of the terms of her contract with us, she would not charge anything for her time. She was terribly modest, she would never recognize that she was good, it was always the horses who had done it. She really was one of the nicest people — and I don't like that word nice — that I have ever met in my life.'

Once during the Tricentrol part of the sponsorship Sally and her husband invited Caroline to dinner after the GLC Clapham Common horse show. They were waiting around trying to get Caroline away but she was always delaying, saying she had to do this and she had to do that for the horses. Finally, as she was preparing to carry two huge water containers from a stand tap to the lorry Sally's husband stepped in with a gallant 'Here, let me do that'.

Sally remembers the incident with a laugh: 'He could hardly lift one, they were so heavy. She let him do it, one at a time, but it was amazing how strong she was. It took some time for my husband to live that one down.'

Very often Sally travelled with Caroline to some of the smaller shows on the English circuit and she remembers how tired Caroline always was. 'We would be sitting in the living quarters of the horse-box chatting and having a cup of coffee and suddenly, just like that, she would be asleep. She had this amazing ability to cat-nap. She was always awake in time for her class but it was obvious she never got enough sleep. When you come to think of it she didn't have time.'

Caroline's sense of responsibility toward her sponsor sometimes went to ridiculous levels. Shortly after the Tricentrol deal was signed the company helped her to acquire a super, all-mod-cons, horsebox that was professionally liveried up in the sponsor's colours. When the box was finally delivered Sally Tooth felt she wanted to give Caroline a little present to go with the lorry and decided on an electric sandwich-making machine for the lorry's kitchen.

'It was the ideal gift for her because she was always cooking something up for the girls, if not in the box then in her little kitchen off the stables at home, and we thought it would help keep the wolf from the door when she was at shows. However when I went up to see her at Priors Marston a little later she was most distressed. Apparently the power supply in the box was such that the toaster could not be operated. Caroline wanted to give it back. Her view was that we had given it to her for the box and, as it could not be used, it would be improper of her to keep it. Naturally I told her not to be so silly and to set it up in her own kitchen if it wouldn't work in the lorry but it was typical of Caroline's integrity that she wanted to give it back because she couldn't used it for the purpose she had been given it. That was Caroline.'

Neither Tricentrol nor Trimoco, who renegotiated the contract when the company reorganized itself and became two separate companies in 1982, were ever put out by being associated with Caroline in what were, by her own high standards anyway, lean years. As Sally Tooth says: 'Both Tricentrol and Trimoco did well from the Caroline Bradley association and people who had never heard of us before would say when hearing our name "oh yes, you're the people who sponsor Caroline Bradley, aren't you?" It is such a shame that, just as the young

Trimoco Rubber Ball and Trimoco Manuel — two of the horses that Caroline had high hopes for after the departure of Tigre.

horses she had worked so hard with were beginning to show results, it all had to end.'

And the work Caroline did put in during that period tended to stretch the imagination.

Ronnie Massarella described one of the days she put in in an attempt to get back to the top.

I had been invited around to their house for dinner but I saw very little of Caroline. In the morning she took six of her younger horses to a show, came back at lunchtime and took six more and then came back again mid-afternoon to take her good horses for the top classes which were at the end of the day. On that day she rode fourteen horses and she didn't get to the dinner table until after nine o'clock at night. Even then she didn't stay long. No sooner had she eaten something than she was back out in the yard. When I left at one in the morning she was still working and you can bet your boots that she didn't get to bed until about three. She was a fantastic girl.

Taking fourteen horses to a show was unusual even for Caroline but she regularly took nine and she rode every one as though it was her first ride of the day, even

though it was often a case of jumping off one and straight into the saddle of another.

In the last year of her life Caroline's work-load increased even more. With Trimoco Manuel and Trimoco Rubber Ball she had a couple of horses that were beginning to win big competitions for her again but she was determined not to be caught out with nothing coming up as she had been with Tigre. She took the better-grade A horses to all the major shows but she never stopped her whirlwind round of the lesser shows with the younger horses. It was a workload that worried her father.

'At the beginning of this year [1983],' he said, 'she told us that she couldn't afford and hadn't the time to take a holiday. It was the worst decision she ever made. She worked herself into the ground.'

Meals were stand-up affairs taken on the run, sleep was something to grab in spare moments and the luxury of an entertainment was out of the question.

During this time she sometimes looked back with nostalgia to the halcyon early days when she only had a couple of horses to think about — as she had when she was first picked for England at the time of the Dublin International in 1966. She never gave up enjoying the life and she never wavered in her conviction that the horse was the most miraculous of animals and a privilege to work with but 'it was more fun in those days because life was so much less complicated'.

To those who didn't know her Caroline was always a picture of health. Tired certainly, and tired mainly through punishing work; never actually ill. But a part of this superfit, dynamo, image was a façade.

Most people in sports that result in lots of bumps and bruises suffer as they get older. Broken bones and dislocations heal quite quickly but, although everything seems fine at the time, there is always a price to pay in later life.

In Caroline's case she had not only been thrown from horses more times than she could remember, and wrenched and twisted and broken her body with frightening regularity, she had also been the filling on numerous occasions between the earth and a half a ton of horse. Never once did she complain and she was always back in the saddle as soon as she could be (sometimes, especially after she had suffered concussion, far quicker than she should have been) but, although the public were never aware of it, she was often in pain.

The price Caroline paid for her crashes was arthritis. It wasn't serious but she was often in pain down her right side and sometimes had to take painkillers just to make riding possible. Despite this she drove herself remorselessly and, in the final few weeks, packed in more shows than was reasonable in her passion for the sport.

There can be no doubt that it was her dedication, her refusal to compromise, her contemptuous disregard for her own pain and her single-minded determination to get back to the very top that eventually killed her.

She arrived at that final show in Ipswich in June 1983 as she had at countless

Opposite
Neatly done — Caroline and Rubber Ball, the last horse she ever rode. His stable name for some unfathomable reason was Tubby

When Tigre went Tricentrol Manuel was his most likely successor. Here Manuel and Caroline show good form over a spread at Charlton Park in 1980. Caroline bought Manuel from Paul Schockemohle and won the Birmingham Grand Prix on him, delighting her sponsors.

others during the weeks leading up to it. With her, in her Trimoco box, were a half dozen or so horses that she loved and planned great things for. She knew them and believed in them. She felt that they had what it took to be stars and she was determined to help them achieve it. If there was a touch of personal ambition as well who could blame her. She loved to win and she wasn't winning as often as she would have liked. She now had horses with that special little dash of magic that could take her there again and she was determined, perhaps too determined, to give them and herself every chance. In her own case it was too much.

The last moments of poor Caroline's life are now painful public knowledge. At the age of thirty-seven she had ridden Trimoco Rubber Ball into second place in the first round of the main jumping competition of the Suffolk Show. She had just dismounted in the collecting ring (it is one of those dreadful ironies that the Suffolk Show had always been one of Caroline's favourites) when she complained of feeling unwell and crumpled to the ground. St John Ambulance men were at her side within minutes and they did all they could but they had no respiration equipment and the kiss of life was not sufficient.

An ambulance was rushed to the scene and she was taken the two miles to Ipswich hospital but she passed away some time during the journey.

Within minutes news of her death had reached every corner of the world and tributes from colleagues and adoring public alike began pouring into the family home.

Opposite
Caroline signs a new three year contract with Tricentrol in January 1982. Standing behind is Roger Smith, the chairman of Tricentrol Motor Corporation Limited, who became one of her closest friends.

In the pain of their grief Mr and Mrs Bradley (along with elder sister Judith who travelled up from her job with National Hunt trainer Josh Gifford to be at her parents' side) began to realize just how deeply Caroline was loved.

Perhaps this is best summed up by the tribute sent by a fan from Dublin. His name was Patrick and he stood at the same place every time the British team appeared at the Dublin showground. He cheered on every rider and always had a special cheer for Caroline. Harvey Smith called him the team mascot. Somehow or other he found out Caroline's address and birthday and, without fail, sent Christmas and birthday flowers to the Bradley home. He was just a show-jumping fan who paid his money at the gate just like everyone else but he, and an army of others all over the world, had fallen in love with her. His letter to Mr and Mrs Bradley when he heard of the death was one of the most moving they received and they knew they were not grieving alone.

But perhaps it was the thousands of little girls with ponies of their own, who dreamed big dreams of being Caroline Bradleys themselves, who suffered most. The feelings of these young girls were very poignantly summed up by a message on a wreath sent to the funeral. It was from twelve-year-old Jane Probert from Selsey in Sussex and she said: 'From a little girl who tries to model her life on yours — I will sadly miss you.' Jane sent her tribute jointly from herself and her pony Stargazer and it wasn't the first time the two of them had been moved to do something for Caroline. Earlier, when Caroline and Trevor Simmons were trying to raise the money to keep Tigre, Jane had sent Caroline £10 as a contribution towards the price!

Jane Probert, and the thousands like her, will continue to model their lives on Caroline Bradley and that must be the most enduring tribute of all.

Caroline herself was the first to help and encourage these young riders. She knew that the British team of the future was growing in the pony clubs and small shows and she was quick to encourage parents to make sacrifices for the sake of their children.

'Fortunately,' Caroline once said, 'anyone who really wants to get into top riding can because there are lots of people who would willingly help a young rider with talent, and it doesn't mean they have to have their own horses. Obviously it is easier if children have parents who buy them a horse but anyone who has got real flair and determination can wriggle their way in somewhere. Horses are expensive to keep but there are an awful lot of people I know who don't earn a fantastic amount of money but who manage to get a good, well-behaved cheap pony for their children. Instead of going out every night or having expensive carpets and so on they scrimp and save to give their children fun.'

Tom and Doreen Bradley did that for her and she couldn't understand why more parents didn't do it for their children. She was always scornful of outward display or needless luxury and was quick to point out the hypocrisy of parents with new cars who said they couldn't afford a pony for their child. She was rightly the Pony Clubbers champion — it will be a long time before they have someone to hold their banner quite so high again.

CHAPTER 8

What Others Said

Alwin Schockemohle, the Olympic Gold medallist and one of show jumping's all-time greats, had no doubts about Caroline Bradley. She was 'the best woman rider in the world'.

Alwin was not prepared to compare Caroline with the Broomes, Smiths, Heins and Wiltfangs of this world — and rightly so because there would have been times when Caroline was ahead and times for all the others too.

He put Caroline firmly in the top élite — the only woman to occupy such a position — but in the world of women riders he had no doubt. She was head and shoulders the best.

Perhaps the best tribute the Schockemohles, as a family, ever paid Caroline was in trusting her to bring on their own young horses. At the time of her death many of the young horses in her Trimoco string were jointly owned by Caroline and Paul: he knew that she had no equal where the youngsters were concerned.

Alwin, of course, had been a child prodigy rider himself and at nineteen had been named in the German squads for both Three-Day Eventing and show jumping for the Stockholm Olympics. He appreciated Caroline's all-round ability as a horsewoman — an ability amply demonstrated by a very creditable sixteenth in the gruelling Badminton Horse Trials of 1969 when she rode Alpaca. This was three years after she first rode for England as a show jumper and it underlines Alwin's opinion that Caroline was the best all-rounder around. 'I don't think any of us really appreciate quite how good she is,' he once said.

Caroline's unofficial business agent Peter Pleasance remembers things about Caroline which sometimes exasperated him but which he recognizes were part of her considerable charm.

My position was unofficial, like everything with Caroline. About five or six years ago we were sitting in the kitchen of my farm in Yorkshire and Caroline was talking about the Blue

Caroline always did all she could for the disabled and was very keen on Riding for the Disabled, which was a way of bringing joy into the lives of people who would otherwise have missed out. Here she gives freely of her time to a group of mentally handicapped children brought to the 1981 Olympia by the Ampthill and District Lions Club

Band advertisement she and the girls had just made. She mentioned how much it had brought into the stable coffers and I said, "oh yes, what about repeat fees". Caroline looked at me blankly and said, "I beg your pardon". She didn't know what I meant and it was typical of her. She was not a businesswoman. She was very good on a horse but had no idea of, and no desire to learn, the ins and outs of the business side. As an advertising man myself, and as Caroline was best friends with my sister in law Celia Raynes, I told her to put any future business dealings on to me for vetting. It all started just like that and, I tell you, there were times when I regretted it.

Peter's problem was that he could never get Caroline to appreciate, or care, that time was money.

If someone rang from the north of England and asked if she would go up to help them with a young horse she would do it. It made her what she was and it was one of the reasons she didn't have an enemy in the world but it appalled the businessman in me.

I know that was Caroline's great charm and I never wanted to take that simple enthusiasm away from her but I wanted to stop her falling into traps — and there are many in business. Right to the end though, even though she was far more professional in business matters then than when I first met her, I had great difficulty in getting her to say 'no'. If a Pony Club clinic wanted her to do a demonstration on how to handle young horses she would always say yes and sometimes travel hundreds of miles to do it. Often she would drive her horses up in the late afternoon, do her demonstration in the evening, and drive back again at night. It would make a hard day even harder for her but she never refused. She loved those Pony Club kids and it was the very stuff of life to help them with their own animals. It wasn't good business but it was Caroline through and through.

One of the greatest tributes to Caroline's ability was paid to her by Roger Smith, the Tricentrol, and the Trimoco, executive who backed her for the original sponsorship. At the time Caroline only had young and unproven horses in the yard and, when the deal was being negotiated, Peter Pleasance told him, 'Look, we can't promise you anything. It may be that after two years we'll still only have a group of Grade C horses doing county shows around the country.'

Roger Smith was undeterred. He had confidence in Caroline and his attitude was to go ahead and put his trust in her. It was a trust, of course, that was well founded. At the end Caroline had six grade A horses in the Trimoco string — a startling performance even in the world of show jumping.

Caroline always felt a deep gratitude to Roger Smith and, as time went by, the businessman/client side of their relationship gave way to a very deep friendship. The friendship extended to Roger's wife and daughter and Caroline became almost another member of the family. The cement of this was in their personalities. Roger committed his company's money on the strength of his belief and Caroline, in her appreciation, struggled to give back everything that she could. Neither of them ever once regretted their association — an almost unheard of state of affairs in the normally rigid and commercially demanding area of advertising sponsorship. That they were able to achieve this mutual trust was a tribute to them both.

For David Broome, who despite Caroline's few moments of misplaced doubt over the Tigre bid remained one of her closest friends on the circuit, Caroline's death was a severe blow.

In a written tribute in his show-jumping column in *Horse and Hound* David spoke of the 'unreal' nature of the loss of Caroline. He was part of that superb Gold Medal-winning team at Aachen and he recalled her pluck and skill in pulling those medal winning clears out of the hat.

'We all had a soft spot for her and she was very good with young people. Whenever she did a course she was perhaps the most popular of all.'

David added: 'The general admiration and love felt for Caroline was shown by the tremendous attendance at her funeral. But if it had been possible to suggest to her that was going to happen she would have answered, "Don't be a b..... fool, I'll be lucky if two people turn up".'

All the members of that Aachen team, David, Derek Ricketts and Malcolm Pyrah, were at the funeral as were most of the top jumpers with whom she had shared her love of horses. Harvey Smith, whose earthy Yorkshire wit and craft Caroline had admired tremendously, was there as was Paddy McMahon (the man who ended up with Tigre) and virtually everyone who had played a part in her life. Lars Sederholm and Peter Robeson who between them fine-tuned her early riding, Dorian Williams, who had known her from her precocious Pony Club days, Trevor Banks, Douglas Bunn, Paul Schockemohle... the list seemed endless.

One of those who was there to pay his last respects to a girl he loved dearly was British Chef d'Equipe Ronnie Massarella.

Caroline rode young horses for me in the early days but I first saw her really riding on her Russian horse Ivanovitch and I thought then she was brilliant. And then I saw her get on to Franco after David Barker but I didn't really get to know her until I took over the team in 1969-1970.

I've got some wonderful memories of her. The amazing thing about her was that she could always put a good round together. In those days we hadn't got all good horses, you never really have. Occasionally you have a top rider without a good horse but they still manange to get the best out of something that was good over national classes but was not quite an international horse and Caroline was just a little bit clever, and brilliant, at extracting the maximum out of them on the occasion.

She was a great team rider. A lot of people laugh at me because I say there are team riders and there are team riders. There are riders who are brilliant in their own right but who become greater when riding under the British flag. There are other riders who are brilliant individuals in Grand Prix but never rise to the occasions when it comes to riding on teams. Caroline was superb. She was like David Broome, Harvey Smith and Derek Ricketts — great riders but always that little bit better as team members.

Like Alwin Schockemohle, Ronnie Massarella was in no doubt about Caroline's eminence in the sport:

I believe, and they can talk about anybody, but in my book she was easily the best lady rider in the world. She was a brilliant, brilliant rider with young horses. She didn't have the money to jump on top horses. She worked her way up the hard way with her own skills that she had worked hard to get. If anyone had anything to say she would listen and she would go home and practise and practise until she had got it right. That's why I say she was the greatest lady rider of all time. She could ride any horse in any type of competition, she knew how to train horses and get horses ready, she knew what muscles to work on and she really understood horses. I know she is compared with Pat Smythe but, for me anyway, Caroline left Pat at the start — her knowledge alone put her in a class apart.

Ronnie believed that, if she had wanted to be, Caroline could have been a millionairess:

I truthfully believe that if I hadn't managed the British team and had managed Caroline instead she could have been worth a million. For her brilliance, her horsemanship and her ladylike ways she was an ideal woman to manage to give sponsors great value for money and they, in turn, would have paid her handsomely.

When I look back I ask myself why I didn't talk to her more about these things but she wasn't easy to talk to. She loved horses, she didn't want to be a millionairess, it wasn't her style. She didn't want to be a star on a pinnacle, she wanted to be there at the grass roots doing the work herself. It wasn't her style to have a lot of people running around doing the work for her — it just wasn't her nature to be like that.

One of the things about Caroline that most endeared her to Mr Massarella was her almost child-like reluctance to be a burden on anyone. In the early days of their relationship Caroline was with the British team in Canada and arrangements had been made for the team to go out to dinner in the evening. When it came time to go everyone was waiting in the bar and Caroline was still in her room. As manager, Ronnie went up to shake her along but when he got there he found her sitting on her bed in her long dress counting her money.

I asked her what she was doing and she said she was seeing if she could afford to go out. I laughed and told her not to worry and that she wouldn't need any money but it was typical of Caroline. She always wanted to pay her way — she hated to think she was getting something for nothing.

She crammed some marvellous moments and years into her life and I shall miss her terribly but I'll tell you this. I believe in afterlife and, in my book, Caroline Bradley is well and truly in Heaven. She never had a bad word to say about anyone and she never did anyone any harm. Losing her is a tragedy.

Ronnie Massarella's views are shared by almost everyone who ever knew Caroline and each of them has a story that sums up what Caroline meant to them.

Liz Richards, who looks after the Public Relations side of things for the British Show Jumping Association, remembers Caroline with particular affection.

I remember once we received a letter from a Lions Club in Wales saying that they were bringing a young girl with spina bifida, who was Caroline Bradley mad, to Birmingham for the Easter Show and would it be possible for her to meet Caroline. I immediately rang Caroline and she said — 'of course I will, just keep reminding me'. Arrangements were made for the young girl to meet Caroline at four in the afternoon at the stables at the show and, at four on the dot, Caroline came charging round on her little motorbike. She spent a full half hour with that child. Manuel and Rubber Ball were brought out of their stalls and Caroline treated the little girl as though they were equals. There was never any feeling that this was a megastar doing a PR exercise. She made that little girl feel ten feet tall and, when she had to leave to go into another class, she gave the girl an Easter Egg and a Trimoco T-shirt. I have never seen a little girl, especially one with something as awful as spina bifida, so happy. All the other riders were around — David Broome, Harvey Smith, the lot — but she had eyes only for Caroline. It was very moving and heart-warming and so typical of Caroline — she just adored children, especially ones who shared her love of horses.

Stories like that abound when people start to talk about Caroline but most of the little pleasures she gave to others — children in particular — happened in private, far away from the glare of publicity. It never occurred to her that a particular action might be 'good for her image' or that she should do this or that for the sake of appearances. Whatever she did, she did because she wanted to, not because she felt she had to.

Caroline never lost this girl-next-door image of herself but, toward the end of her life, she became much more self-assured and confident as a professional.

As Peter Pleasance says:

Paul Schockemohle had interests in about five of the horses in the Trimoco string and he was sending young horses to her all the time because of her special talent. Caroline, of

course, could tell straight away if a horse was going to be good or not and she knew that Manuel was one with unusual potential. In the early days she would have said nothing about this but, with the maturity and confidence she gained with the years, she knew she had to 'bite the bullet' and do something about it.

One afternoon, while pacing out a track at a show with Paul she asked whether he wanted to sell Manuel. Paul said yes and, before they had time to get back to the collecting ring, a price was arranged.

It was inspired. Within a month or so she had taken that horse to Birmingham and won a Grand Prix. We were all delighted. After having thought we might have to wait years for a top grade A horse we now found ourselves with one in months. Indeed most of the horses she had picked out as showing potential were beginning to show it by the end — that is really the cruelty of it all.

Journalists, who usually tend to be a bit cynical when heaps of praise are showered upon someone from people in the same sport, sometimes thought that Caroline was too good, too wholesome, too sporting to be true, but whenever this was put to Caroline she puffed it away.

'Rot,' she once said. 'You should hear me when I come out of the ring after having jumped badly on a good horse. I can be very short indeed and woe betide anyone who comes up and tries to tell me what I have done wrong.'

Ronnie Massarella recalls this side of her character clearly:

She was no shrinking violet. She called a spade a spade and there were times when we had our disagreements — especially at times I left her off the team when she felt she should have been included. She tended to brood a bit and get herself down in the dumps but the boys could usually bring her out of it. When they ribbed her a bit at dinner after that bad first round in Aachen she was sullen at first but then she rose to it and grabbed Malcolm Pyrah round the neck so tightly that blood flowed. It wasn't much but her own blood was up then and there wasn't anyone at that table who wasn't certain that Caroline was going to pull something out of the hat the next day.

In a newspaper tribute to her after her death *The Times*, too, was quite unstinting:

Life was not easy for her with no one 'on the ground' to advise and help her, but she was dedicated to her sport, throve on hard work in unbelievable quantities, combined with hours and hours at the steering wheel of her lorry, and despite some terrible falls she seemed to have inexhaustible reserves of courage and strength which enabled her to overcome every difficulty.

Without doubt she was far and away the most outstanding woman rider of show jumpers in the world. She kept her own counsel and her qualities of character brought a unique distinction and dignity to show jumping. She was the pattern for young aspirants and she will be quite irreplaceable.

Caroline's groom Mandy Barber lost more than a former boss; she lost one of her three best friends. As Tigre's groom Mandy helped Caroline through the trauma of the sale and she sat with Caroline for mile upon mile as they drove from show to show on the European circuit.

Opposite
Just a few days before she died. Caroline and Manuel at the Herts Show, 1983

It was very tiring and we used to chat to stay awake but I would always fall off to sleep and Caroline would hit me with a newspaper or something to wake me up.

She was one of the most hardworking and dedicated people I have ever known but she had great difficulty expressing her feelings — even to me. With me it didn't matter, of course, because we were close enough to know what each other was thinking but getting across to anyone else was painfully difficult for her.

But painful or not Caroline got across to the world with her actions; she didn't really need her words.

Perhaps the views of all those who knew her, whether just as a shy but talented rider on their TV screens or as a personal friend, was best summed up by former BBC commentator Dorian Williams who gave the address at Caroline's funeral service.

Dorian said:

In less than twenty years Caroline brought more happiness and more pleasure to more people than most of us will ever do in a lifetime. Before she was even forty her successes were acclaimed all over the world — a source of enormous pride to her family and those closest to her and those who worked with her.

And for the rest of us a source of profound gratitude. By her performance she showed that it does not matter who you are — if you have a natural skill and determination you can get to the top.

The shock of Caroline's death will pass and the sadness will pass leaving us with a great pride and a great gratitude for all the pleasure and happiness and inspiration that Caroline, in her short life, gave to so many thousands of people.

But the best insight into what made Caroline Bradley what she was came from her own mouth. At a show in 1980 she mentioned that Franco, that wonderful old horse of Robert Hanson's which, at fourteen, had taken the 21-year-old Caroline to her first Grand Prix successes, had died peacefully at home.

'He was only twenty-six and fit right up to the end. It was a terrible loss. He's buried in his favourite spot — I couldn't send him for cats' meat, I respected him too much.'

That Caroline Bradley respected all her horses is something that nobody who had anything to do with her — no matter how insignificant and no matter from what distance — could ever doubt.

APPENDIX

Nations Cup appearances for Great Britain

Year	Place	Horse	Faults per Round		
1967	Olsztyn	Franco	0	4	
	Leipzig	Franco	0	0	
	Dublin	Franco	8	4	
1968	Lucerne	Franco	16	11½	
1969	Rome	Franco	8¼	8	
1970	Aachen	Franco	4	NS	
1971	Lisbon	Wood Nymph	4	4	
1973	Nice - Ladies European Championships	True Lass	7¼	5¼	
1974	Vienna - Ladies World Championships	True Lass	Finished 2nd		
	La Baule	True Lass	Finished 4th		
1975	Geneva	True Lass	0	0	
1976	Rotterdam	Marius	5	4	
	Paris	Marius	4	4	
1977	RIHS Hickstead	Marius	8	0	
	Geneva	Marius	4½	0	
	Dublin	Marius	8	0	
	Rotterdam	Marius	0	12	
1978	Nice	Tigre	4	4	
	St Gallen	Berna	4	12	
	Aachen	Tigre	0	8	
	Hickstead	Tigre	0	4	
	Aachen - World Championships	Tigre	13·35	¼	0
			(team Gold Medal)		
	Calgary (Canada)	Tigre	0	0	
1979	Geneva	Marius	4	0	
	Paris	Tigre	0	4	4
	Hickstead	Tigre	8	0	
	Rotterdam - European Championships	Tigre	5·05	0	8
			(team Gold Medal)		
	Calgary	Marius	8	8	
1980	Paris	Tigre	0	0	
	Dublin	Tigre	4	0	
1981	New York	Tricentrol Manuel	0	0	
	Toronto	Tricentrol Manuel	4	8	4